THE MESSENGER

The Messenger

FRIENDSHIP, FAITH,
AND FINDING ONE'S WAY

Douglas John Hall

CASCADE *Books* · Eugene, Oregon

THE MESSENGER
Friendship, Faith, and Finding One's Way

Cascade Books
A Division of Wipf and Stock Publishers
199 W. 8th Ave., Suite 3
Eugene, OR 97401

www.wipfandstock.com

ISBN 13: 978-1-61097-317-5

Cataloging-in-Publication data:

Hall, Douglas John, 1928–
The messenger : friendship, faith, and finding one's way / Douglas John Hall.

ISBN 13: 978-1-61097-317-5

xii + 168 p. ; 21.5 cm.

1. Miller, Robert Whitely (1924–2005). 2. Student Christian Movement. I. Title.

BS H 2011

Manufactured in the U.S.A.

*This book is dedicated
to all those
unsung
messengers and mentors
who discern in others
the capacity for
understanding
and
service.*

. . . and how shall they hear
without a messenger . . . ?

ROMANS 10:14

Ironic points of light
Flash out wherever the Just
Exchange their messages:

W. H. AUDEN
["SEPTEMBER 1, 1939"]

Contents

Preface

THIS IS A BOOK about a friend—but a friend who was also more than a friend: a friend who was a messenger.

Friends enhance one's life, messengers change one's life. Or, more accurately, one's life is changed by the messages they bring. In theory, the messages are strictly separable from the ones who bring them; but in practice, I've come to think, it is very hard to sustain this distinction. For the message is never just a matter of words. The messenger in some way embodies the message—though he or she may also in some way obscure it. In any case, even after more than sixty years I cannot *quite* separate the message from the one who first conveyed it to me in a convincing way. So this little book is about him—Bob Miller.

It is also, of course, and quite inevitably, about the one to whom this messenger communicated the message he was given to bring: myself. As I look back over the pages I have written here, I realize—with some embarrassment, to be honest—that I am myself often present in them. I can only beg the reader's indulgence by noting a certain truth that is contained in the metaphor as such: messages are not only conveyed by someone, they are intended for someone. Had I conceived of this task as a biography of my friend (which it certainly is not!) I should myself have stayed strictly in the background. At least that is what all great biographers imagine they are doing! But because I could only write about my friend in the way that he was actually present to me over the course of six decades, I had to adopt this metaphor—the messenger. For that is who he was, for me.

It is a wonderful metaphor, and one that shows up in many cultures and languages. Think of Mercury–Hermes! It is prominent in the Bible. There, sometimes, messengers are called straightforwardly messengers; but sometimes they are called angels (the word *angel* simply *means* "messenger"), at other times they are called preachers or prophets or wise teachers; sometimes they are just mysterious strangers who join people as they walk along a road, or sit pondering the meaning of events. On occasion they may be nothing more than disembodied voices, speaking out of burning bushes or other "natural" phenomena—donkeys, even! But usually, in biblical literature, they are human beings—just ordinary people with 'all their warts,' speaking or gesturing or in other ways trying to get their messages across to other ordinary people with all *their* warts!

But this little book is not just about the messenger, who was also my friend, and me, the receiver of the message, whose whole life was turned around because of it. It is also about the times during which my friend and I lived—well, since I am still living it would be more accurate to say the times during which he lived. To be quite specific, that means between the years 1919 and 2003. If you pause to reflect on those numbers, you will realize how important a role *time* has to play in these reflections of mine. The year 1919, you will recall, occurred just after the close of what in my youth we called the Great War. Very soon there was another and (some say) even greater war. Life all over the planet was thrown into chaos by these wars: *our* lives, Bob Miller's and mine, were not left untouched by these events, though we were by no means at the centre of the storm. But the Great Depression of the 1930s came closer to us, and so did the aftermath of World War II, especially in Bob Miller's life. I will argue here, however, that an even more decisive time for the living of *our* lives, especially his, was the period we call the sixties.

There are, then, three points of focus in this story: the life of the Messenger, the life of the one receiving the message, and the times in which this giving and receiving occurred. "The Moment," as Kierkegaard might have said.

But the *hidden* theme of the story is *the message itself.*

I fear, *entre nous,* that that theme may in fact be *too* hidden—obscured by all the details of life, the dates and places and names of persons who walk in and out of this account. Nevertheless, it is there. And I think the discerning reader will easily discover it. If you do not, please get in touch with me. I can provide a whole reading-list for you!

D. J. H.
Notre-Dame-de-Grace, Montreal
April 2010

1

Beausoleil 1948

WE SAT RIGHT AT the edge of the lake, the three of us. The great folds of granite were warm from the August sun. After all, the island was called *Beausoleil*, "beautiful sun," and most summers it lived up to its name. For young men and women who spent their working lives in Toronto offices it was a vacation paradise, if only for a week or two. It was that for me, too—though as a south-western Ontario village boy, present among these city-dwellers through an odd constellation of relationships, the setting was less novel. What was new for me was finding myself among members of my own generation, some of whom had become tentative friends from the summer before. At work in the business office of the newspaper of our country-town 'down south' I was the youngster amongst ten or fifteen older men and women, little more than an office-boy in fact, though I'd been put in charge of 'classified advertising.' Last summer's brief discovery of the joys of being with contemporaries had whetted my appetite for more. This summer, however—the summer of 1948—was proving to be a little different. The difference was made mainly by the presence of three people, six or eight years older than most of us. I'd never met them before. Between them, they were to alter the direction of my young life.

ere all just back from the Canadian West, where they
nt by the Home Missions Board of our denomination,
Church of Canada. It was the policy of the church to
ordained ministers and their families in congrega-
—— that were regarded as missions because they were remote
and could not employ ministers on a regular, salaried basis. Many,
if not most, of these congregations were located in the Canadian
West—especially the three prairie provinces. Two of my new acquaintances were a young married couple, Arthur and Margaret
(Meg) Young, who had been in the Peace River Country of northern Alberta for five years. Their year-old toddler, Patrick, was with
them. They were returning now to Toronto, where both had been
graduate students, Arthur at Emmanuel College and Meg the University of Toronto's School of Social work. They would take up
ministerial responsibilities on Toronto's east side. Arthur was to be
the assistant to the well-known Ray McCleary, long-time minister
of WoodGreen United Church on Queen Street near Broadview,
and much-honoured senior chaplain during World War II. King
George the Sixth had himself pinned the medallion of the Order
of the British Empire on Ray's uniform.

The other "new guy" was a tall, athletic young clergyman
named Robert Whiteley Miller. He had graduated from Emmanuel College in 1946, and had just finished a two-year 'stint'
on a mission field in Shellbrook, Saskatchewan. He'd just become
twenty-nine, and was on his way to Edinburgh where he would
undertake a year of post-graduate study at New College as recipient of Emmanuel's travelling fellowship. He had been awarded this
much-coveted scholarship as one of the most promising student
of his graduating class, though he had spent only one year at Emmanuel, the first two of the three-year Bachelor of Divinity degree
course having been taken at the internationally renowned Union
Theological Seminary in New York City. The death of his salesman
father had occasioned Bob's return to his native Toronto to complete the church's requirements for ordination.

Ray McCleary himself spent a day or two at the camp that
summer. He was the most remarkable United Church minister I

have ever known. As the brochure of the *Ray McCleary Towers* rightly claims, this genial bachelor cleric who never lost his North-of-Ireland accent and rarely appeared in public without a clerical collar, possessed "phenomenal organizational talents and charismatic leadership." It was those qualities that enabled him in his mid-sixties, as his own life was ebbing away (too soon), to establish a residence for needy seniors in Toronto's east end. If you consult the Internet you might think that the 'Ray McCleary Towers' are the only way Dr Ray McCleary is remembered today. But that was only one of McCleary's projects. In the late 1940s McClearly had raised enough money to build and administer the Wood-Green Community Centre as one of the many kinds of outreach of WoodGreen United Church on Toronto's east side—a modern, multipurpose building with facilities for all ages and interests. To walk down Queen Street East with Ray McCleary was an experience in itself. Every street-cleaner, every kid, every drunk, every ex-con, every old lady or gentleman knew him. And he knew them—by name! He was a regular visitor to nearby Don Jail, and his good friends ranged from businessmen to intellectuals, from the very poor to the very rich. He had an uncanny ability to see the potentiality for good in people, and he could inspire groups of many types and purposes—service clubs, the YMCA, sports associations, and of course his own congregation with its varied activities. There was about him a refreshing *joie de vivre* that set him apart from most clergy and encouraged people of every walk of life to trust him, seek his help, and share with him their deepest hopes and fears. He was a good friend of Sir George McLeod, founder of the Iona Community, and his own ideas of Christian community, which he tried to incorporate at WoodGreen Centre, were similar to Sir George's. People who had long since lost touch with the church brought their babies to be baptized by him, their young to be married, their dead to be buried. Ray, they knew, wouldn't turn them away, though he might lament their break with the church. In short, as the Germans would say, Ray McCleary was *ein Mensch*—a real human being!

And he was the reason for our being there on the island of the 'beautiful sun' in Georgian Bay just off Honey Harbour. In one way and another, we were all part of Ray's flock: the thirty or so young women and men who were members of WoodGreen's Young People's Union, the Youngs and Bob Miller who were known to Ray from their years at Emmanuel College, which was also *his* alma mater, and I too, an outsider who was there because the Martin family, which was very active in WoodGreen Church, happened to have a cousin in my village near Woodstock who was a particularly good friend. The camp on Beausoleil was itself available to us because Ray McCleary was a trusted friend of the Lions Club of Toronto, which owned and operated this camp chiefly for city children who needed to be rescued from the humid heat and noise of "Toronto the Good" (as it could still be called in 1948)! The young people from WoodGreen were, most of them, boys and girls who had grown up in the vicinity of the old church that bore the names of two of its previous clergy, Reverend Messrs Wood and Green[1] Now they were between the ages of eighteen and thirty-five. Most were not university graduates, but they had acquired training and expertise in various business and professional fields, and were already skilled and successful young adults who were at the same time loyal members of the church. (Readers who are too young to have experienced Canadian church-and-society prior to 1960 may have difficulty picturing such a group, because (in Canada as in Europe) very few successful twenty- or thirty-year-old business and professional singles are to be found in most big city congregations today. This already says something about the socio-historical context that is the background for my memories of Bob Miller. It should also be noted that 1948 was only three years after the cessation of the terrible conflagration that we call World War II.)

With his remarkable sense of timing and planning and human relations, Ray McCleary had commandeered the Youngs and Bob Miller to provide leadership for the two-weeks on Beausoleil that summer. Bob was in charge of the study and worship sessions,

1. Hence the spelling WoodGreen—though in more recent times this has given way to Woodgreen.

which were normally held out of doors; and the Youngs, who would now become part of the ministry at WoodGreen, were there chiefly, I think, to become acquainted with some of the younger members of their congregation.

2

With that bit of background, let me return to the homely scene with which I began. Seated on the warm granite rocks just outside the main hall of the camp that day, three of us—Meg Young, Bob Miller, and I—were enjoying the quiet after the happy rowdiness of after-breakfast singing in the dining hall of the camp (Whatever became of those marvellous old camp songs?—"They built the ship Titanic . . . , and it was sad when the great ship went down," or 'What's the use of wearing braces?"—the Woad Song, to the tune of *Men of Harlech*). Bob and Meg had both been students at 'Vic' (Victoria College in the University of Toronto) and knew one another well. I, of course, knew neither of them, nor they me. But for reasons I hardly understood myself I was drawn to them. As I listened to Bob's study/worship meditations and heard snippets of conversation between him and the Youngs, I realized that I was being given a peek inside a world hitherto foreign to me, but one that seemed strangely alluring and important. It certainly wasn't just that they were both unusually attractive people, though they were; my desire to know more of them stemmed from something much deeper. But in order to try to explain what that deeper thing was I shall have to say more about myself than I should like to do in an essay dedicated to the memory of someone else. Perhaps, however, if I reveal enough about myself at that stage in my life I will also, indirectly, find a way to speak about Bob Miller. The truth is, I wouldn't be able to say what I want to say about Bob in this attempt at a 'profile' without, in the process, revealing more about myself than I would ordinarily like to do. Our knowledge of others is always partial at most, but where it is genuine it is also knowledge gained in and through *relationship*. My approach here, therefore, will be to introduce Bob Miller to the reader in the way that I myself came to know him. I will reserve some of the more 'objective' material—his parentage, education, and *curriculum vitae*—for later.

Clearly, I was at a juncture in my own life that summer when I was unusually—let us say—open to suggestion. I had just become twenty. For four years I had worked in the business office of *The Woodstock Sentinel-Review*, one of Lord (Roy) Thomson's Canadian dailies. I loved being part of that newspaper world, and I've never regretted that I hadn't been able to finish high school but had my real education among a group of intelligent, dedicated, and generous office people, men and women who were glad to take a 16-year-old under their wings and help him deal with the surprisingly complex world of business and society in small-city Canada during and immediately after World War II. My hard-working parents needed some financial contribution to the family from the eldest of their six children; so I left the Woodstock Collegiate Institute after Grade X and enrolled in a one-year course offered by the small Woodstock Business College. When I graduated from that institution in the Spring of 1944, I had considerable proficiency in bookkeeping, shorthand and typing, so I was able to find a job fairly soon.

Being on the whole mature for my years, as well as ready and willing to learn, I gained the confidence of my co-workers and superiors after a year or so, and found myself very much part of the company of the fifty or sixty men and women comprising the staff of our county-town's daily newspaper. It was an excellent place from which to learn the inner workings of Oxford County and its prosperous and historic little capital, Woodstock. Founded (officially!) in the early 1830s by Queen Victoria's cousin, Rear Admiral Henry VanSittart, Woodstock boasted many beautiful old mansions and considered itself "the dairy capital of Canada." My mother's ancestors had been in the city and its surroundings much longer than Admiral VanSittart and his influential friends, but since they were not retired army or naval officers or owners of great mansions, they didn't qualify as founding figures.

Though my wages at *The Sentinel* were ridiculously low by today's standards (I started at sixteen dollars a week), I enjoyed my work and the people of my workplace immensely, and since I lived at home (which at that time was in the village of Innerkip, seven miles from Woodstock) I was even able to save a little money for my *real* objective in life.

That objective was the serious study of music. No thanks to myself, I had been born with an exceptional ear for harmony, melody and the seemingly infinite progressions of sound, and my greatest wish was to perfect these gifts sufficiently to give my inherent drive to compose music enough sophistication to satisfy at least my own sense of beauty and worth—and maybe even become a source of livelihood. I realized, of course, that my real enjoyment of life at *The Sentinel-Review* was in considerable part because I did not think of that work as permanent. The money that I saved during the four years I'd been there, which was little enough even for the 'forties,' I intended to use, eventually, to study piano and composition seriously and full-time. But I had begun to wonder how, exactly, that goal would ever be attained.

At the same time, another whole area of consciousness was claiming more and more of my attention. For whatever reasons— was it the war? or the kind of exposure to the raw facts of life and death that is unavoidable in village life? or the continuous struggle of human beings to live and work together without unceasing conflict (my office experience)? Or was it simply the business of growing up and discovering both the possibilities and the limitations of human existence?—for *whatever* reasons, I was besieged by a questioning mind that was never satisfied with easy answers. Later, after many years of study, reading and simply living, I would realize that during these adolescent and early adult years my mind was being invaded by all the great questions: the ethical ones, of course (what is *good*?), the epistemological ones (how do we *know* anything?), the teleological ones (what is the *purpose* of all this striving?), and the most elusive of them all—the *ontological* question: what does it mean to "be"—and its dark antithesis, what does it mean *not* to be. Like Hamlet: "To be, or not to be . . ."

My friends often told me: 'Forget it! Just *be*. These questions of yours have no answers anyway! You're just making life difficult for yourself. Enjoy your youth, you won't get a second chance." Fortunately there were one or two who listened—one in particular: the aforementioned cousin of the Martin family of Wood-Green Church in Toronto, an unforgettable and empathetic young woman a few years my senior, who was, I fully suspect, an angel in disguise—a messenger in her own right. Her name (of blessed memory) was Gertrude Barker.

The church, which in those far-off days was the centre of our village life, was of course the logical place for the exploration of such questions; but apart from that young woman and two or three others I found the church of my childhood and youth too obsessed with matters of personal morality to manifest any interest in my kinds of questions. Until 1925, it had been a Methodist congregation, and an all-too-characteristic moral piety, amounting to petty moralism among the more vociferous church members, dominated the discourse of the community, including its prayers, preaching, and Christian education (i.e., Sunday school). One got the impression that being a Christian, if it didn't mean simply refraining from strong drink, tobacco, and other such abominations, meant striving to be "good" in the manner generally agreed upon in our village culture. In other words, it was a watered-down and simplistic version of John Wesley's doctrine of perfection. Jesus was the model of this moral perfection towards which we were supposed to struggle—the Jesus of Warner Sallman's *Head of Christ*, which hung in our sanctuary as it hung in nearly every other Protestant church on the continent. I felt I could never achieve such an ideal. As, years later, a famous New York professor of mine put it, this well-known "Jesus as Example" conception of Christian morality was like holding up an ostrich-egg to a bantam hen and commanding, "Do your best!"

Not that I was opposed to the idea of being good. I really admired good people—*really* good ones, like the aforementioned angel in disguise. But I did *not* admire the moral smugness that passed for goodness among the most influential members of our church and Sunday school (everybody went to Sunday school back then). Besides the fact that much of that "goodness" was petty and consisted chiefly of the avoidance of certain "sins," there was always an undertone of hypocrisy in it. *Hypocrisy* was a word that I heard often in my youth. It was a favourite term of my father, whose manner of life (he drank!) greatly displeased the church pillars. My father noted that the most notoriously "good" were characteristically the most financially secure of the community, and were often involved in questionable business and personal dealings. Such dealings could not be entirely concealed in a village of three-hundred souls.

Beyond that, as I moved into the mid-teens I found myself increasingly disillusioned with *my own* feeble attempts at being a kind, helpful, considerate individual—a 'good boy.' Why, I wondered, did I take such inordinate pleasure and pride in my *good* deeds? What did Christianity have to say about *that*—the propensity of the good to false moral superiority? Pride. *Hubris*—as I learned to call it later. If Christianity is no more profound than that, if its highest wisdom is the call to a superior "righteousness," then, I thought, it hasn't gone very deeply into the dark, subtle places of the human spirit.

Fortunately this moralism of my religious community was countered—it seemed to me—by some things that I heard from the Bible. In those far-off days, even in liberal denominations like ours, the Bible was still quite prominent. Of course its more radical teachings, such as its whole critique of "religion," were obscured by the religious presuppositions we were conditioned to bring to the Bible, including the very questionable ideas we had of its "holiness." But if one had ears to hear, the Bible's often startlingly *unchurchly* counsels sometimes broke through the church's rhetorical but ineffectual insistence upon its sacredness. "Why do you call me *good*?" Jesus demanded of someone who saluted him as 'Good Teacher' (Matthew 19:17). And, strangely, "goodness" seemed to be the chief concern, not of Jesus, but on the contrary of some of those whom Jesus regularly criticized—like the Pharisee who, praying to God in the temple, praised himself for being so much better than "this publican" (Luke 18:10–11). Beyond that, he seemed to be more at home with "bad" people and social out-casts—the despised tax-collector Zachaeus, the woman "caught in adultery," and so on.

And then there was this odd business of "faith"—Paul's spe-ciality! (Yes, we even got into the Pauline epistles in Sunday schools, back then). "You are justified by faith, *not by works lest anyone should boast*" (Ephesians 2:9). What an argument I had that day with our (very moral) Sunday school teacher! He was perhaps the *chief* pillar of the church, and he showed himself that day to be a staunch disciple of the Epistle of St. James. "Faith *without works*," he impressed upon me, "is *dead*" (James 2:20).

But while my suspicion that Christianity went farther than morality was evoked by these provocative scriptural allusions, I found no echo of this suspicion in the religious context in which I lived—an avowedly *Christian* context. Most of my contemporaries didn't even notice passages like Paul's famous definition of *justi-fication*; most of the elders were obviously content with "higher righteousness"; and the various ministers who came along to our small congregation, with one possible exception, were as puzzled by my questions as I was. Even the dear, aforementioned angel who patiently listened (for hours!) to my quibbles, seemed unable to set me straight. Where my youthful "religious quest" was con-cerned, I felt frankly very much alone—though I was not 'a loner' in other respects.

And then in the summer of 1948 I found myself in what seemed an entirely new and different kind of Christian commu-nity. These people—and especially the three clergy, Ray McCleary, Art Young, and Bob Miller—didn't seem particularly interested in Christian morality and piety. They were all decent men, but they didn't go on about their decency. I knew that the leading lights of my village church would have found them all quite doubtful, as they had found the one clergyman to whom I alluded earlier, the one "possible exception": he hadn't "lasted long," as people said. I myself didn't know quite what to make of these new acquaintanc-es, but I heard and saw enough of them to want very badly to know more about *their* Christianity. And I also knew, or thought I knew, that they would be ready to hear my unquenchable questions.

And *that*, of course, was why I pursued Bob Miller and Meg Young so shamelessly that day, when it was obvious that Bob really wanted to read the book he had in his hands. I don't know what words and "sighs too deep for words" poured forth from my pent-up young psyche that day—I know I talked a good deal. I'm sure my stream-of-consciousness outpourings had a lot to do with the aforementioned questions—the ethical, the teleological, the ontological and so forth—in their most untutored and naïve forms. And I remember being rather annoyed that Bob Miller seemed almost to ignore my outburst altogether! Maddeningly, he kept repeating a sentence from the book that he was reading. Every time I stopped for breath, he'd drag out that wretched sentence again. I don't think I understood a word of it! And I still don't remember what its point was. I wish I did! I think the book was by somebody called . . . Karl Barth.

But while I'd be glad enough to know these details, they didn't matter, in the end. What mattered was the whole scene, and the thoughts and emotions that it evoked in me. Perhaps in a manner similar to the Zen masters, and perhaps not, Miller was confronting me with a piece of wisdom far beyond my capacity to grasp. Perhaps it was this very silencing of my incessant and probably incoherent twenty-year-old babbling—this almost total disregard for my self-important grasping for "answers"—that took me so by surprise that I had to "think again," or perhaps stop thinking long enough to listen. Perhaps it was the stillness of the morning, the warmth of the ancient rock, the immensity of the lake and sky—the 'beautiful sun' . . . Who knows? It was all of these things, I guess—and more. Much more. But it remains in my mind as a moment of calm and resolution, defying "answers" and leaving in their place still greater questions; but questions that I might now, perhaps, entertain with a certain courage, even a certain exhilaration.

Of course this moment does not stand alone. There were the twice-daily meditations, among other things. I listened to them with new interest: what would this 'different' young minister say?—what that could possibly hold the rapt attention of a group of street-smart young men and women? He always began with a biblical text. Obviously he had thought beforehand about what he wanted to say to us, but there were pauses—hesitations that sometimes left you wondering whether he'd find the next words. Like the others, I had of course heard scriptural homilies before, but this was something else. It certainly wasn't great oratory. Clustered together at the shore early in the morning or as the sun was setting, our little group would not have been moved by oratory, even if it were good oratory (which oratory, in our experience, seldom was!). Bob Miller spoke quietly and without histrionics of any kind. Yet the whole event produced in us—certainly in me, but I think in all of us—the impression that we were being involved in something very serious. The biblical words were not framed in the usual aura of cushioning sanctity. One felt the more or less familiar words of Jesus's parables or Paul's theological meditations were addressed to one's own life in all its ambiguity and nakedness. Watches were not consulted; no one fidgeted or looked bored. When, on the last day, Bob Miller reminded us that we had been living for this brief period on an island, and that such life was always a bit artificial however idyllic, and that now we had to leave the quiet beauty of this *Beausoleil* and go back into the demanding and confusing world, and that that would be where the depth of our faith, hope and love would be tested, we were none of us, I think, quite ready to leave. We'd have been glad enough to listen to many more such meditations

But I haven't yet mentioned the stories. For sleeping, we were divided into smaller groups, each group housed in a cabin with individual bunks. The unmistakable if somewhat sanitized odor of urine made it obvious that these huts in the woods were normally used by little kids. Of course there was no electricity, so when the seven or eight of us in the cabin to which I was assigned turned in for the night, we were engulfed in darkness. I don't know how it came about exactly, but on the first night Bob Miller, who was in our cabin, asked if we would like to hear some stories. What? Bedtime stories for business and professional men in their twenties? I couldn't believe it! But my skepticism vanished as the storyteller began, in a low, unhurried voice, to tell us tales of the sort that might have been strictly for children but contained, in subtle ways, suggestive depths of meaning that were beyond the average child's comprehension—mythic stories that used religious themes and allusions to convey thoughts that transcended most of what passes for religion.

As I learned much later in life, the stories Bob told were based on a collection called *Christ Legends* by the famous Swedish author Selma Lagerloef—the first woman to receive (in 1909) the Nobel Prize in literature. Lagerloef gathered these legends from many European sources, and then gave them her special twist—which I would say was a unique blend of creation mysticism and Lutheran Christology. So, for instance, in one of the most memorable of the legends, the robin, created by God as a small *grey* bird but told by its maker that its name (which it was sternly admonished by its Maker strictly to remember) was "Robin Red Breast," finally got its red breast when, in its fellow-creaturely feeling for a poor man suffering on a cross, it found that some of the blood of the crucified one had stuck to its little breast. Another told of how the donkey got its long ears (because it had to have its ears pulled so often when its Maker tried to get it to listen to Him) . . . and so forth.

I was amazed—and as I remember these evening stories more than sixty years later I am *still* amazed—at the effect they produced in all of us young men, sophisticated according to our own lights and swaggering like all the others in our own circles, yet still children enough to follow these legends with rapt attention. There wasn't a sound in the little house. When the storyteller stopped speaking a thought-filled silence prevailed. Persons who knew Bob Miller only in contexts of theological, biblical or artistic discourse might well have been surprised had they heard him at his storytelling in that dark forest hut.

I realize that I am spending a good deal of time on this initial meeting with the Reverend Robert W. Miller, but I have had to conclude, over the years, that I was given an impression of him during those few days that rarely surfaced in later life. Perhaps it was one of the results of his having been pastor of a small rural parish during the two previous years. Perhaps it had to assume a less prominent—even, it may be, a hidden—form as he made his way back into the world of the academics and the activists. It's possible he may even have lost touch with that dimension of his personality, that particular talent, though I am told that he loved to tell stories in the student work-camps that he organized later on. In any case, I think that what Bob Miller revealed to us about himself in his storytelling was as much his true self as any of the more analytical, didactic, or organizational aspects of his later life. For me, his *charisma*, which was many-sided, manifested itself more immediately in those deeply engrossing retellings of Selma Lagerloef's legends than in any of the other ways in which I experienced him.

There is one more component of this first meeting that I shall have to relate if what follows is to make sense. As I indicated earlier, my great ambition at this stage was to become a composer of music. I improvised regularly at the piano, and I had composed several pieces of music—most of them not actually written down. One of these (I thought of it as a tone poem) was a rather complicated piano composition that I called *The Sea*. Perhaps ironically, I had never yet seen the sea when, at age seventeen, I began to compose this piece. But I had what I suppose may be a kind of aboriginal conception of the ocean—after all, it's the matrix of our existence! My piece had a theme that was clearly influenced by two composers whom I admired a great deal: Rachmaninoff and Brahms. Technically it was difficult because of swift passages and rolling arpeggios for the left hand. For that reason I can't play the original version of it today with my arthritic fingers—though I revised it recently as a piece for an old man: *The Sea Remembered,* so to speak. But in 1948 I loved to play it for others, and very often I found Bob Miller sitting in the shadows and listening with what I thought was special interest.

It was with deep regret that I had to part from my friends of Beusoleil that summer, and especially from Bob Miller. He was bound for Scotland a few days after we all made our way back to

Toronto, and I assumed that I would never meet him again—that this meeting, however meaningful it had been for me, would soon fade into the background. Though a little reluctantly, I was ready to return to my desk in *The Sentinel-Review* and the companionship of my honest fellow-workers there. The experience in Georgian Bay had, however, kindled anew my desire to get on with the vocation that I believed was my real destiny, far off and vague as it seemed.

3

I had been back at work only two or three weeks when, quite out of the blue one day, I received a long-distance telephone call. It was Ray McCleary phoning from Toronto: "*We* think," he announced, "that you should now come to Toronto and study music. I've found part-time work for you at the Broadview YMCA, and with some evening work at the WoodGreen Centre you will make enough to pay for your lessons at the Royal Conservatory. You can live with the Martin family, who will be glad to give you a place for the same amount of board as their own working children pay. So there you are! It's all arranged. Pack your bags, and come along as soon as you can!" McCleary never did things by halves, and I am sure that both Bob Miller and Arthur Young were included in that royal "*We* think . . . " that prefaced all these arrangements.

There was no point in hesitating. I left *The Sentinel* with the blessings of all my co-workers there. The only person who questioned my decision was my grandmother, who felt I had made a very good place for myself in the local world of business, and that I ought to remain where I had a real chance of advancement instead of following a hunch and a dream. But soon I was registered with an excellent teacher at the Royal Conservatory, getting to know my fellow-employees in two small business offices, and learning how to find my way around in 'the big city.' I practiced the piano at WoodGreen Church every morning and began to attend Conservatory classes in counterpoint, harmony and other aspects of musical theory as well as music history. The great Healy Willan lectured in counterpoint, and Godfrey Ridout taught the history of Western music. I had no time for frills, but I did manage to get seasons' tickets for the Toronto Symphony concerts at old Massey Hall—twelve concerts for twelve dollars (in the peanut gallery, of course). And I never missed a Sunday, or a Young Peoples' meeting at the church. Art Young always preached at the Sunday evening services, and his sermons were literary masterpieces with real substance. With his and Meg's encouragement, Ray's cheerful presence, and the wonderful home setting of the Martin family, I felt I had entered a new world—though I was homesick sometimes, too.

About a month after my arrival in Toronto, Meg Young came to church one Sunday morning with a letter for me. It was from Bob Miller, now beginning his studies in Edinburgh. It came as a complete surprise—but a happy one. "Just a line of welcome to you on coming to Toronto," he wrote, and "Congratulations on your beginning at the Conservatory . . ."

> Things won't always go as they should, but I hope that they go well enough to keep you somewhere in sight of things. Hope that you will keep me in touch with how you get along . . .
>
> I suppose everything at the Conservatory is very frightening. Everyone will seem so important and busy and wise. They aren't really, you know. After you are there for a while you will begin to be important and busy and wise too, and will frighten other little people who come in for the first time. You will know of course that you yourself are not wise and important, and that will make you begin to suspect that most of these other wise and important ones are not either.

He had, he said, a special request of me: would I please send him a copy of *The Sea*. "I can't play," he wrote, "but I will be able to find people who can. You can think it over."

I did send him a copy of *The Sea,* and a recording of it as well. He showed it to a professional musician he had met, an organist in one of the large Edinburgh churches, and this generous man studied my manuscript and sent me an appreciative though critical assessment. He recognized my love of Rachmaninoff, but felt that was all right; however I did need, he said, to develop the main theme of the piece more fully.

Bob's next letter contained more information about his life in Edinburgh and his struggles as a graduate student. I was surprised by his modesty.

> I was just thinking that our situations are really quite similar. You see, by your standards I know quite a bit, but here I am amongst a great and wise people who have a great store of factual knowledge about theology, church history, peoples' teachings, etc., which I do not have to the same extent, and which, since I am here as a graduate student, is something of a disadvantage for me.

Languages, he continued, especially Greek and German were a particular weakness. "I hope to spend some time in Switzerland before I return, as that is really the Protestant Church's theological heart and mind, and I could not feel right having come so close and not going. That means a good knowledge of German is necessary, so I am at work. But I feel like a neophyte among the ancients, and without much time."

Evidently Bob was experiencing a challenge greater than he had had to face earlier, and it involved more than a lack of factual and technical knowledge:

> What we are always looking for really, and often subconsciously, is security. That sense of being in the right, and being alright, of being accepted and having an assured position both in regard to our particular job and in regard to our friends. Some people are more bothered by the insecurity of their life than others. Some even enjoy it, but not most of us. I suppose that insecurity goes along with our self-concern, that is our selfishness, for if we were ever rid of the one we would be rid of the other. We are always more concerned about our security with our fellows than about our security with God; the one seems near and pressing and the other far away. And we have to find our way from our social insecurity to the fact of our insecurity before God,

and that this is what underlies and disturbs and upsets both
us and all men [*sic*], and that only He can act to alter that,
and that therefore we have to have from Him His promise
of security, of forgiveness. And that we really must have it
for ourselves, we must really be certain of it, and of it alone.
[*Letter of Nov. 13, 1948, from Edinburgh*]

In spite of his high-sounding praise of the "great and wise
people" in Edinburgh, I had the definite impression, which was
later confirmed in conversation, that Bob Miller was in fact not
terribly enthralled with the situation there. His next longer letter gave his address as "Alumneum, Basel, Switzerland," though
he began by stating that he was writing it in Holland—undoubtedly from the home of his good friend, Ellen Flesseman–van Leer,
whom he knew at Union Seminary in New York, and about whom
I shall have more to say later on. He had left Edinburgh, he said,
in mid-March, 1950, and did not intend to return there until the
summer, when (as he thought then) he would be on his way back
to Canada. "I am going to remain now for the rest of my studying time over here in Switzerland. That is the place for which I
really headed when coming over and now I will really begin to
work there." He wouldn't be able, he said, to write to me often,
because he'd have to spend all the time he could find concentrating
on German. He did not say that these lectures would be by Karl
Barth, chiefly—after all, at this stage I had little if any awareness
of such luminaries in the world of theology. He was living, as I
learned later, in a residence whose don or supervisor was another
well-known Basel theologian, Oscar Cullmann. Cullmann, who
originated in Alsace, and who recently (2009) died in his nineties,
never achieved the fame of Barth, but he wrote several influential
books, including *Christ and Time*, and established a reputation for
ecumenical diplomacy between Protestants and Catholics. Karl
Barth once told him, "On your tombstone, Oscar, they will write
'Advisor to Three Popes.'" With his sister, the bachelor Cullmann
presided over a student home. Bob Miller told me later that he
had had to sit at Cullmann's right hand, at table, and listen to the
exploits and achievements of the great man. "I've never met such

an egotist," said Bob, who rarely allowed himself any such negative statements about others. Several years later, when I was a graduate student at Union Seminary, Oscar Cullmann came to give the Hewitt Lectures, and he appeared on the platform of the main lecture hall dressed in a purple academic robe with all his medals displayed across his chest. John Coleman Bennett, who introduced him, wore a plain charcoal-grey suit. A standing joke of the period, in theological circles, has Herr Professor Doctor Cullmann asking everyone, "Haben Sie mein Buch gelesen?" [Have you read my book?]

The lectures at Basel were complex and linguistically difficult. I only heard Bob speak German, very briefly, on one occasion, and at that time I was myself only a beginner in the use of that language. Since he was in continental Europe only for two years, at a maximum, I doubt very much that he had attained *great* fluency in German. There were obviously moments of great discouragement: "I find it very easy to just stop trying to understand and let the whole thing go by as un-understandable. It is easy enough to do that in English, let alone in German too."

Evidently in my previous letter to him (I do not have copies of what I wrote to him), I had been airing my old problem: how to be a reasonably decent person without in the process letting one's (relative!) goodness and decency become a matter of pride and false superiority. In responding to this, Bob Miller suggested that perhaps the real problem for me was a sense of *inferiority*. "I wonder if you don't have a feeling of inferiority and being out of place, which is compensated for in you by a knowledge that you are superior to others in many things and ways. So that you wander back and forth from superiority to inferiority, from self-confidence to uncertainty. No man is completely one or the other of these, no matter how much the appearances may seem to say so. Somewhere hidden he has the other side . . . like two sides of a coin; but the coin always does have two sides."

> There is no direct way out of the difficulty, because by overcoming the one side there is always the other side ready to turn itself up to the light. So it can only be a constant

sea-saw. The only way of meeting the difficulty is by turning
to a third thing. We cannot keep a balance between the two
sides of the coin. It has to balance on something else. That
means in one sense a work of some kind to which we give
ourselves—that is a quite practical thing.

I didn't feel that this analysis quite met my concern, though
it was interesting enough as a commentary on the superiority/in-
feriority dialectic. Probably at this stage I didn't possess concepts
and language adequate to the articulation of my struggle, but what
I was wrestling with was the ancient problem of *superbia*, pride,
and the manner in which the very *quest* for "righteousness" (to
use the biblical term) continuously got in the way of actually *feeling* "right" about oneself—got in the way of *authenticity*. Ironically,
when one spent so much effort *striving* to be "acceptable" and "secure" (words Bob had used earlier), the very striving precluded
the attainment of what one strove for. What I needed to hear,
obviously, was that acceptance, security, authenticity—in biblical
terms, *justification*—could only come to one as a gift, a matter of
grace. "We are justified by grace, through faith, not by works lest
any one should boast"—the central message of the Reformation
about which I had argued with my Sunday School superintendent.
I think that I was *almost* on the verge of believing that, just then,
but I needed someone to say it to me . . . *out loud.*

In the next long paragraphs of the same letter, the one written
in Holland, Bob Miller began to move in that direction:

> About faith, to continue with the illustration you give me: if
> we have faith in a medicine, there is no possibility of over-
> confidence in ourselves developing, for the faith is not in
> ourselves but in the medicine. The medicine would be the
> only one who could develop an over-confidence! The very
> fact that we have faith in a medicine indicates it would be
> impossible for us to have over-confidence in ourselves,
> because it indicates there is something wrong with us, so
> that we need a medicine. Our faith no longer now can be
> in ourselves, it must now be in the medicine. It is like a
> man who is healthy and does not need any medicine and is

always prating about his health and physique, etc., and the same man when he is not so healthy any more and must rely upon a medicine to keep himself in trim. Now he can no longer prate about himself, and must prate about his medicine.

You ask how we get faith, and there is only one answer to that: from God. You get faith in a medicine only from the medicine and only as you use the medicine. You get faith in God only from God and only as you make use of Him for it, come to Him for it. The Christian church says there is but one place to get it, and one place to make use of it, Jesus Christ and the Bible. The medicine has come, as it were, to us. It is like the man (above) whose security or faith is now no longer in himself and his own health, but in his medicine and its ability to keep him healthy.

Apropos my concern that our 'good deeds' too easily feed our egos, Bob's response was that "Perhaps it is God's way of prodding us to go out of our way to do a good deed occasionally that we have a nice warm feeling after it." I had heard that line before, and I found it rather shallow; but the letter-writer went on to something better, it seemed to me:

Certainly neither the commandments, nor the parables, nor the teachings of Jesus would give you a leg to stand on in not lending a helping hand where needed. The way that they would guard you against your feelings of self-satisfaction is not by telling you not to do these things, but by telling you that you ought to have done them much sooner, that you ought not to have needed to find your fellow in distress before you helped him, that you have left undone countless things that you ought to have done, in fact that you learn, even from your good deeds, what a heel you are. And also that in that way you learn how you never do any completely good deed. The goodness of a deed lying more in the motive than in the act itself, and none of our motives are ever unmixed, nor completely good. If we take a feeling of pleasure after such a deed as a reward from God to US for OUR doing SUCH a good deed, then we will end up a

worse heel than ever; but if we see it as but a stirring and
prodding and luring us on to go out of our way to assist
the need of others—even to the point of its costing something—that is different.

Perhaps the most pertinent counsel of this long letter from
Leiden, however, came in the concluding paragraph; for there it
became obvious to me that Bob Miller was chiding me (and, may
I say, a good deal of old and new liberal, pietistic Christianity in
general!) for putting such uncritical emphasis upon my own "feelings." Here it becomes clear that the message of the Reformers
(and of Karl Barth their contemporary champion) had profoundly
influenced the thinking of the thirty-year-old:

> As Christians, we have to learn about these things not from
> our own feelings, or from our weighing of them, but from
> God. That our actions may be determined more and more
> by Him and less and less by ourselves. Had God taken your
> line there would have been no crucifixion or birth of Christ,
> nor even any creation in the beginning. There was nothing
> to compel Him to share with us at any point. But He did,
> and so must we learn. Our life is exactly the opposite of
> sharing and is centred in self; for God this is quite a justifi-
> able position; for us it is completely unjustified. We learn
> from our little good deeds how really the whole meaning
> and purpose originally of our life was in just such sharing
> and living together, and we also learn how far we are from
> being that and how in any complete and full sense life such
> as that is now impossible for us, as we are. [*Letter of March
> 26, 1949*]

I remember that I pored over this letter a good deal. About
this time, I think, my preoccupation with music began gradually to
give way to a more inclusive, if also elusive, compulsion to *understand*. I found myself needing to *know* more! I felt that I knew next
to nothing. Arthur Young's sermons helped a good deal, as did discussions with him and other friends, like my beloved Martins. But
I knew that I needed to go more deeply than I had ever gone before—more deeply than brief sermons and haphazard discussions

could take me. Alone in my room at night, I began to read the Bible more seriously than I had ever done before. Following a hunch and snippets of conversation from the past, I turned to a biblical writing that almost didn't make it into the canon: *Koheleth*—the little document that came to be called Ecclesiastes, rather strangely. I remember thinking: "If this kind of honesty, including this honest *doubt*, can be found in this book, I had better consider other parts of it again." I went from Ecclesiastes to the Gospel of St. John with the same sense of reading these often familiar words for the first time. Intuiting that I needed to learn how to read serious philosophic work, I went to the Broadview Library and got out William James's *The Varieties of Religious Experience*. I hardly understood a word of it, but I persevered. I went with the Youngs to hear Willem Visser 't Hooft, a Christian thinker and ecumenist whom I would later come to admire greatly. I knew that he was saying important things. I also knew that I didn't follow him very well.

Perhaps the most significant breakthrough at this juncture in my "pilgrimage" came when I heard, for the first time, J. S. Bach's *St Matthew Passion*. It was performed by the Mendelssohn Choir and the Toronto Symphony Orchestra, conducted by the great musician who altered Canadian musical taste in the middle of the twentieth century: Sir Ernest MacMillan. It was a marvel, to me. Lois Marshall sang the soprano parts. Greta Kraus was at the harpsichord. I sat there enthralled, not only with the music, but with the text as well—and the inseparability of the two. If ever I needed to realize how close music and theology were—the two things, as Luther said, that keep the devil at bay!—this spring 1949 performance of the *Matthaeus Passion* was an unforgettable lesson. Subconsciously, I think, it was then that I 'decided' that a move from music to theology would at least not be a non sequitur.

But at that point it was certainly not a matter of *decision*. The whole WoodGreen experience, the exposure to great music and to close friendships, and (above all) the letters of Bob Miller were undoubtedly pushing me into a new vocational direction; but there were still many bridges to cross. Fortunately, the letters from Europe kept coming. The next one had been written in Geneva on July 28th, 1949. The term in Basel had ended, and Bob was staying briefly with a friend before moving on to Germany, where he would remain throughout the summer and until resumption of classes in Basel in October. "I am afraid that my German sounds like anything but a native—in fact a native might have a hard time recognizing my German. It comes slowly. I will be attending a summer course at Heidelberg University which I trust will help it along for our fall term."

In this letter he takes up, once again, the theme of faith. I suppose I must have responded to his earlier remarks on that subject by writing about the difficulty I was having even in understanding the *meaning* of the term faith, let alone experiencing faith. He wrote:

> The poverty of our faith will always be a problem for us, I suppose; but somehow we go on believing, and that is the wonder. Perhaps we should spend less time worrying about not believing and concern ourselves with the tasks we have to do, and with the places where God promises that He will help us to believe, or even more give to us the faith which we do not have: prayer, the Bible, Jesus Christ, the church and the Sacraments. We all of us have a place in which we are to be obedient and follow out the will of God for us, and it is the smallness of our obedience which troubles us and perhaps also causes the problem of faith. Perhaps if we could do better with obedience, faith would not be such a problem, because they are not really two things but one. It is an obedience which can be stated first and most simply in the commandments, and stronger and more directly in the N.T. And then these must secondly become quite concrete and specific for us in our own life, with our own talents.

I must also have referred to my discovery of Ecclesiastes, because the letter moves from this quite Calvinistic affirmation of the inseparability of faith and obedience to a commentary on "vanity." I realized, reading it, that Bob Miller was concerned lest I become so enamored of Koheleth's "All is vanity" that I could end in cynicism! Barth's 'triumph of grace' rings audibly throughout the following paragraphs:

> Because vanity is inseparably bound up with my very inmost being, then I can never find anything that is not vanity, for I can never find anything without myself being there. I cannot leave myself behind to find something, and that would be the only way I could find something without vanity. But God can give us something without vanity because it is He who does that, not I. And He can give me anything and all things when and where He will. But in the end what God would give is Himself. That is, He would not be apart from what He gives. He would not give "something" to me, but would give Himself, so that the Giver and what is Given remain together and are not separate, and then also so that He Who[ever] receives, receives not a separate gift, but becomes identified with the gift and the Giver. God the Father is the Giver, God the Son is the Given, God the Holy Spirit is the receiver, and by Him and in Him I am included.
>
> This is all theologically spoken, but it is that which happens, we cannot say where or when, we can only say that we believe it does and has and we go on with what we have to do believing that it also will happen both in small and invisible ways now and also in a great and visible final act when all will be fulfilled. Music can perhaps be a means of the happening now—God being willing, and also a witness to the happening then—God being willing.
>
> If this is muggy, I will blame the weather for it is muggy tonight. The sea breezes do not reach this far into town. I should not say sea breezes for it is only a lake, but a very beautiful one. The town lies between the lake and the mountains, and the cathedral high on a hill in the middle of the town watches over it in good Calvinistic fashion. This was the first real Protestant city in the world, and to it refugees from all Europe fled the Roman Church. It is the centre of all sorts of international organizations now, from the League of Nations to the World Council of Churches.

It is entirely probable that these thoughts did seem somewhat "muggy" to me as I pondered them in Innerkip in July of 1949. Both the author's Trinitarian language and his evident enjoyment of Calvin's Geneva were quite foreign to me at that stage, and even today, though for other reasons, I do not feel quite at home with either this language or the implicit adulation of Calvin. *Then* I just didn't feel terribly touched by what Bob wrote about "obedience"; *now* I find it much too "theocentric" in an abstract sort of way— lacking in a "point of contact" (to use a loaded term!) with human experience and feeling.[2]

2. In the years between "then" and "now," I came to understand this Barthian/Calvinist language very well indeed—maybe too well. It is heady stuff, and one can slip into the use of it simply by being surrounded by literature and by others who use the same language. But as I was exposed more and more to the theological *critique* of this "Barthian" language, especially the critiques of my great teachers Reinhold Niebuhr and Paul Tillich, but also many others, I realized that while it is a highly exhilarating mode of thought and speech so long as one remains within the circle of its practitioners, it fails to communicate with those who find themselves outside this circle. *And one is oneself always, with at least part of one's consciousness and experience, outside that circle.*

In other words, in my subsequent life and work as a theologian I came to feel, gradually but with increasing acuteness, the gulf between this intense and intensely captivating Christian discourse, based on a triumphant theology of grace and a revelational "positivism" (Bonhoeffer), "beautiful" as it was in the all-embracing "Dogmatic" of Karl Barth, absolutely failed as *apologia*—that is, as a language Christians could use in their struggle to communicate "Good News" *to the world*, including "the world" within themselves. Emil Brunner, I finally felt after much wrestling with him, was right in insisting, over against Karl Barth, that there needed to be a "point of contact" (*Ankneupfungspunkt*) between the Gospel and those for whom the gospel is intended.

And as I reflect on the life of my friend Robert Miller, I wonder very seriously whether he did not eventually reach that same conclusion—though perhaps only implicitly; or perhaps, even, without fully coming to terms with such a conclusion. Since *his* vocation, unlike mine as a professional theologian, did not involve the need to articulate his belief so explicitly as I, I suspect that he simply *moved into a less fideistic, more apologetic mode in his actual life and ministry.* He could never have become the avid student of modern literature and of ancient and modern art that he was had he held so steadfastly to the kerygmatic mentality that is expressed in these paragraphs.

These compunctions didn't really matter very much at the time, however, because in the meantime I had made a momentous decision: I would enter the ministry. The thought had been in the back of my mind for a long time, actually, but it seemed futile because I knew that I did not have the necessary academic background for such a pursuit. From a purely statistical point of view, I was a 'high-school drop-out.' To be sure, I had put in two years of formal study following my departure from the Woodstock Collegiate, one at Business College and one at the Royal Conservatory of Music. But these, I knew, would not suffice as high-school equivalents, and even with them I would be one year short, since in Ontario at that time there were *five* years of secondary school.

Then one night after an intense discussion in the living-room of the Youngs on Bolton Avenue, Arthur asked me, "Have you ever thought of entering the ministry?" I answered at once that I had, but that I had suppressed the idea in view of my lack of qualifications for university work. Arthur Young had done some of his undergraduate work at the University of Western Ontario in London, and he had heard, he said, that 'Western' was beginning an experiment in accepting "on probation" a few "mature students." He would write to the registrar of the university, he offered, and see what could be done.

Within two or three weeks there was an encouraging response from Helen Allison, Registrar at the U. W. O. There seemed enough promise in my high school, business college and conservatory grades to consider me a candidate for the 'mature student' category. I should come to the university in late August to sit for various intelligence and other tests, and if the results were satisfactory I could be allowed to register for first year on a trial basis. (Later on, the mature student category was adopted by many universities in Canada, but at this point it was still very closely monitored.)

I was elated—though I tried not to be presumptuous. I left Toronto in the Spring, returned to my home in Innerkip, and through my Dad's influence got a job on the CPR Railroad—physically the hardest bit of work I have ever had to do. I spent all my non-working hours reading as widely as I could—Shakespeare, biographies (three of them were of Luther), even grammars.

One of the first tasks I realized I must do was to write to Bob Miller and tell him of my decision. I was a little nervous about that. Obviously his friendship and example had played a significant role in this vocational choice. It had not been made out of any disillusionment with music, or the prospects of succeeding in some aspect of that art; even today that I think that I might well have had a good and meaningful life as a musician—music has remained a love of my life all the way through. But the Christian faith had come to play such a vital place in my thinking that I could no longer consider it in merely avocational terms. The greatest doubt I entertained in coming to the decision for Christian ministry was the possibility that I had been inordinately swayed by the influence of the three clergy who had entered my life a year earlier—Ray Mc-Cleary, Arthur Young, and Bob Miller. Miller especially.

So I wrote to him in Switzerland in some such words as these: "I have decided to become a candidate for the ministry of the United Church, provided I am accepted for study at the University in London, and while I know perfectly well that you have influenced this decision I would like you to know that I intend to go through with it *whether or not you approve.*"

Bob Miller was away from Basel all that summer, and I didn't have an answer to my letter until October (1949). In the meantime, I had taken the two days of tests prescribed by the university, and to my profound relief and satisfaction had been admitted to a probationary year of study in "general arts with theological options," the latter to be taken at the Anglican theological college, Huron College, that was the mother institution of the university. I was already hard at work when the important letter from Basel arrived.

"I am very sorry not to have written you sooner, because your letter really deserved better than this. I have just read it through again, and it is a good letter. Your decision, of course, highly pleases me, and not less so because it did not, and does not, come too easily."

Then, characteristically, as I came to realize, he went on to caution me—rightly!—about certain tendencies he perceived in my character: "One thing to be said is that you will always be somewhat too introspective and full of fears and doubts and questionings about what you do or say. Just because this has its value, it becomes a temptation to some of us. I would say to you now, the more that you can get away from such introspection and questioning and get on with the job at hand, the better. The more we can substitute the searching of the Bible for the searching of our own philosophy, the better."

The next sentence was, as it turned out, a clue to the changes that were occurring in Bob Miller's conception of his own vocation: "Your 'working on the railroad' was a very good thing." He continues—

> It is my opinion that at least for the time that you are studying arts you should not go on a church field but always to some kind of work where you are with people who have to work and work hard and unpleasantly all their lives. These are the people that we need to get to know, factory workers, etc. And that as far as possible you make yourself one with these people, not just in their work but in their play, etc., and not let too many scruples stand in the way. This is a speaking in the dark, but don't you need to become more sure of yourself in your relations with other people, especially young people, and perhaps especially fellows of your own age, so that you can be with them and at the same time be free and somewhat independent of them? And don't lose your music altogether. It gave us some pleasure, even when it wasn't the most perfect, and even if it did sound somewhat like Rachmaninoff—we didn't know the difference.

"By now," he wrote, "you will be well into your first year's work, and finding some of the drudgery it contains . . ."

> I'm glad to see that you are taking Greek from the beginning; never let up on it till you have reached the point that you would rather read the New Testament in Greek than in English—and I mean that! And read as widely and as

much as you possibly can: novels, poetry, philosophy, politics. These next three or four years are the time when you have to lay in this background for the more intensive and specialized work that will follow, and all these are ways of becoming part of the world in which we live, and of the [people] that live in it.

And don't think of the ministry always in too personal terms. There is a job to be done, the church is desperately in need of ministers, *especially of beings who can think, and who are alive to this world, and who having learned the message of the Word can really speak it in the world.*

The letter goes on, then, to reveal some of the influences that were shaping Bob's own future ministry. After some weeks of language study at Heidelberg, he had attended two important conferences sponsored by the Protestant church in Germany, one for medics and one for factory workers.

The latter was especially interesting and led me into some of the problems of the workers and the trade union movement in Germany today. There are approximately 1,000 refugees from the east coming into Germany every day, and you can imagine the confusion and misery that brings in their lives and into the life of an already chaotic and overcrowded country. I visited one of the camps where these people live while a place is found for them to go, four or five families all living in one large room of a barracks. Thousands of people are permanent tramps with no home, youngsters with no parents living somewhat like animals on what they can find or steal. I often wondered how the whole country did not sink into complete chaos under the whole business. It is impossible to believe that in a short twenty years people could go through all the experiences that they have had in Germany, and then today to stand on the brink of a fearful and unknown future. But I must go off to bed now.

Bob's next letter, dated January 15, 1950, and typewritten as usual, began with a handwritten "<u>warning</u> to be read first": "*This seems to be an epistle filled with advice and of such you should ever be suspicious."* It *was* filled with advice, too—most of it good advice, I would say; but the first bit of counsel was somewhat off the mark. I had written to him, I think, about my classes in apologetics with bishop William Hallam, a wonderful, learned Englishman who had come to teach at Huron College after his retirement from the episcopate in Saskatchewan. I greatly admired the bishop's wisdom and his teaching, and my praise of him seemed to irk Bob Miller—I think it brought out Bob's very Protestant suspicion of authority, though it also smacks of his peculiar sense of humor: "Beware of these bishops, son! (The paternal tone is adopted in case you have become so used to listening to them that no one gets your ear any more unless he sounds like bishop himself)"—

> We have a few questions, from the Bible, that we must put to our Anglican brethren before we can be too enthusiastic about their many virtues. The very fact that we would want to begin all our discussion with them from the Bible, and carry it on on that ground alone—that would already be a little disturbing, narrow-minded, unchurchly, unhistorical, etc., etc. to a great many of them. In fact to their history as a church, and the central doctrine of their ministry, and more than all else, their central doctrine of tradition. This latter is the hard nut that stands between us and all the so-called Catholic churches. And on it many Anglicans stand at least much closer to the Roman church than to the Protestant.

I was ready to grant this criticism of "High Church" Anglicans—and there were one or two of them among the theological students at Huron College, but Bob knew little about Huron Diocese at this point, or he would have realized that it was one of the "lowest" in the country. As for Bishop Hallam, he was (as I said in my address to the 2009 convocation of Huron when I was given an honourary doctorate) "the only bishop I have known who could wear, on occasion, pantaloons and silver-buckled shoes and gaiters, and seem entirely authentic." Most of my classes in the theological disciplines at Huron College were of a very high caliber, and prepared me remarkably well for later work in theology.

The next piece of advice from Basel was more appropriate. I can't think what prompted it—perhaps I had been complaining that too much time and energy was spent in futile discussions; in any case my mentor declared, "for goodness sake don't be afraid of enjoying yourself too much in such discussions and thinking. It would be a pretty poor theologian who did not find the chief joy of his life to be exactly there in his theological labours—for us that means primarily the labours that the Bible and the Word that it speaks to us lay upon us. Just be a little afraid of being so ruled by your enjoyments that discipline is sacrificed and order flies out the window and it is no longer the Word Himself Who is the driving motive and real enjoyment, but your own appetite for enjoyment, and this becomes merely a means of satisfying it. Then He no longer rules—but you yourself rule yourself. Thank goodness He is around to bring us to task now and then." The advice is pertinent, but I can't help marveling—today, at least—at the almost archaic-sounding language in which it is stated. The Reformed world of Protestant Switzerland seems to have captivated Robert Miller at this stage of his European experience more than at any other point. It is quite probable that I accepted this language more enthusiastically in 1950 than I could later on. In retrospect, I feel glad that Bob's theological sensitivity was being shaped, as well, by his growing experience of the complicated world in which he found himself. Yet it should not be forgotten (and I will comment later on this point) that the understanding of Christian ministry that Bob Miller would come to embrace grew out of this same very Biblical and Reformation theological thinking. It was not a consequence of the Liberal Social Gospel but of the renewal of critical Protestant thought stimulated by Karl Barth and other architects of the so-called Neo-Orthodox movement.

Precisely that point is demonstrated by the next "advice of which I should be suspicious!"—what to read: "I have pretty well lost contact with things to read at home [in Canada]. I would certainly suggest some reading of Dostoevsky somewhere along the line, especially *The Brothers Karamazov*. Heinrich Vogel *Iron*

Ration of a Christian is good if you can find it anywhere. Dietrich Bonhoeffer—something about Discipleship . . ."

Interestingly, Art Young had already sent me Bonhoeffer's *The Cost of Discipleship* during the summer of 1949, prior to my acceptance at Western. It is perhaps difficult today for students of modern Christianity to realize that in 1949 Dietrich Bonhoeffer was still an unknown name in the Anglo-Saxon world. The copy of *The Cost of Discipleship* that Arthur Young mailed to me in Innerkip that summer is probably one of the hundred or so copies of that book that circulated in Canada at that time. It was the first explicitly theological book that I had ever read, and it made an enormous impression on me—as anyone who knows my own writing will realize. The bibliographic advice goes on—

> Someday you would [be well advised] to read Kierkegaard, though it is perhaps early (*Training in Christianity* might be a good beginning.) Some time too take a look at Karl Barth—*Credo* or *Dogmatics in Outline*. Don't forget Karl Marx. What you should do now is to read as widely as possible, also some of the better modern novels and biography writers. Don't rush out tomorrow and try to read those books I mentioned, but keep them in mind and when you have the chance sample them. They are the sort of things that you can never be sure when you are ready for till you actually really stumble upon the fact that they have something to say to you. The door doesn't always open on the first try, but the room is worth making the effort again. I enjoyed T. E. Lawrence's *Seven Pillars of Wisdom* tremendously once, also Merejkowski's *Leonardo d' Vinci*. Don't let anyone try to talk you out of buying Calvin's *Institutes of the Christian Religion* and beginning the reading of them one of these days. You'll be in the woods a long time, but the more trees you can notice along the way the sooner you will come out. On the one hand, don't try and rush yourself too fast, ahead of what you can understand in your reading; on the other don't compromise too easily with what you can easily understand. But above all don't let yourself be tied to a text-book and examination routine. You must

pass, yes, but these years are your chance to reach out into the thought world which is all around and which can serve immeasurably in the future. Two of the great questions that will surround our lifetimes' work are Communism and Romanism, [so] along the way try to pick up as much of a real understanding for what they are, what they are after, why they should have an appeal in this world. Once I get under way I can go on handing out advice at great length! I had better take a little of it myself and sign off here. Listen carefully to all advice that [people] give you, but keep the salt of yourself free from it. Don't stumble over your own earnestness; it's better to laugh at it.

The spring of 1950 saw Bob Miller in Germany at work among the refugees from Eastern Europe who were pouring into the West in order to escape the real and imagined horrors of Stalinist Russia or simply to find a place to live when their homelands had been utterly destroyed. I do not know this for certain, but I have the impression that, while not weary with his studies in Basel, Bob felt drawn to put into practice the theological-ethical perspective that his educational experience in Europe had accentuated. North Americans, spared the grosser negations of World War II, tend to forget that Europe was still in ruins in 1950—and long after that date. I first visited Western Europe in 1959, and most countries there—Germany in particular—were still trying to rise out of the ashes. 'The German Phoenix'—the economic miracle that made Germany strong again, and eventually the strongest of all—was not in evidence until the 1960s and beyond. When Bob Miller went to southern Germany to work in 1950, that country was still very much a beaten, broken land, struggling to find a way out of the ruins that were the consequence of its ultra-national *hubris*. The Protestant church's work among the victims of the war was centred in Bad Boll, cite of a famous medieval spa in the state of Wuerttemberg. It was there, in the nineteenth century, that pastor Johan Christoph Blumhardt and his son Christoph Friedrich had established their ministry of evangelism and healing.

The Blumhardts are rather unknown figures in the Anglo-Saxon world, but the fact is that they anticipated very much that has occurred in Christian thinking throughout the past hundred and fifty years. Their theology combined a characteristically Lutheran piety with a strong social consciousness that has often been obscured by the doctrinal preoccupations of post-Reformation Lutheranism. They developed an eschatological approach to faith which understood the work of the Christ as a victory hidden by the seeming reign of sin, evil and death yet in reality bringing to bear on the present possibilities for change that transcend the apparent 'inevitabilities' of historical cause and effect. Theirs was indeed a theology of *hope*; and it is not surprising that Jürgen Moltmann, the most prominent "theologian of hope" in the twentieth century and beyond, acknowledges that his own development of this theological tradition relies on the Blumhardts' interpretation as it enters into dialogue with the later Marxist thought of Ernst Bloch. The Blumhardts profoundly influenced the whole 'Neo-Orthodox' revolution in Christian theology, particularly the "theology of crisis" or "dialectical theology," as the early work of Karl Barth is frequently designated. It is no accident, therefore, that after his months of study in Barth's Basel Bob Miller was moved to attach himself to the church's work in Bad Boll.

His first letter to me from Bad Boll is dated June 24, 1950. By that time I had completed my first (crucial!) year at Western. I had graduated with grades that astonished me (I had no idea then that I had any real academic potential), and, in part recalling Bob Miller's advice that I make a greater effort to seek out my own generational cohort, I had joined the University Naval Training Division and was in the midst of my first summer as a cadet at Esquimalt, BC. "How does it feel being a sailor?" he asked. "I sure wish that I could see a real body of water. Here in southern Germany there is nothing of the kind."

The letter goes on to register something of the bewilderment the young Canadian was experiencing as he encountered the chaos and suffering of post-war Germany, with its hoards of "displaced persons."[3] The week before he wrote it, he said, he had had to go back to Switzerland briefly—"and that was a pleasant change."

> Whenever I come out of Germany it is like coming into the fresh air where I can breathe deeply again. The atmosphere and attitude and surroundings are all so different. Here [in Germany] the cities are ruins, the people are in rags and tatters, but even more there is a heaviness and depression over everything that catches me as soon as I come in. The burden of the past and the fear of the future lies heavy on the people here, to say nothing of the difficulties of plain every-day living. The difficulties are all underlined by the 12 million refugees who are perched all over trying to find a hole into which they can burrow, and someplace where they can earn their daily bread.

The physical degradations of the situation, he goes on to say, though terrible in themselves, are less devastating than the demoralized and defeated attitudes of the people. It is that sense of fatalism and meaninglessness that the work of the Christian mission has chiefly to counter—and yet precisely that mission is jeopardized by the very bureaucracy that is supposed to facilitate it!—

3. A friend of Bob Miller's and of Rhoda's and mine was one of the fourteen million refugees under discussion: Maria Fuerstenwald, former professor of German literature and history at the University of British Columbia. remembers the flight to the West vividly. Her close friend Margaret Prang writes: Maria was "one of those 14 million refugees, mostly women and children from eastern Europe (Poland in her case) fleeing west before the oncoming Russians whose official policy of 'loot and rape' was already well known. She carried nothing except a pillow case and a spoon, in case she found someone with food. She considered herself lucky to end up in the British zone with a job as a laundress for a group of army officers. The 'Limey' boss of six laundresses called them 'my bloody Germans' but treated them well, and they got one hot meal a day and some soap, a very scarce item . . . Eventually M made her way to Goettingen and managed to find where the rest of her family was: her father and brother in concentration camps in Poland, her mother trying to get near them to bring them food, another brother just released from the German army and proud of the fact that he had managed to avoid aiming a gun at anyone! What chaos the whole of Europe was in those times" (e-mail message, May 2010).

It is very difficult to make contact with people here in Bad
Boll. They are hidden behind so many layers of resentment,
bitterness, fear, mistrust, etc., that it often takes a while to
get them opened up. That is perhaps the chief purpose of
this whole enterprise, in that it gives the people a chance to
take a deep breath, to hear something else than the pressure
of their daily labours, to contact other people as people. It
is so here that the movement has grown so important that
the leaders are so busy they have little time for the people
themselves who come here, and so are in danger of losing
the point of the whole thing. That is a common German
failing. They work with great industry and enterprise on
something so that it becomes so big and important that
gradually the point of the whole thing is lost in the general
commotion. Here in the AK that is where I come in, for my
chief job is just to be amongst the people, to get to know
them, be their friend and engage in conversation with them
on everything possible. Now and then I give a lecture, and
also help with the general planning, etc. I am one of a staff
of four here who run things. Next week I have to set out on
a round of visits to factories, to which the workers who were
here last week invited me, and that should be interesting.

There was little opportunity for personal diversion or pleasure in this situation—or even, says the conscientious scholar, for
pursuing one's own study and meditation. He had spent an hour
or two lying in the sun that day, he said, and "got myself all red and
tired out." He had rejoiced in the hillsides covered with cherry and
apple trees had been able on a walk to "take a handful" of the delicious fruit whenever he felt like it; but this one "lazy day," even to
the writing of his letter to me, seemed to the thirty-year-old minister "an escape." He ought, he wrote, to be working at the tasks that
give one the wherewithal for one's ministry. But since no-one beyond oneself insists on this, one's own resolve too easily fails. So . . .

"Let me advise you to create for yourself now all the self-
discipline that you can, down to the very smallest point. I
am old enough now to feel already the softening tugs of age
[he was 31!!], when one wants to relax and have it pleasant.

> My discipline fails most of all in the reading of the Bible,
> which was never a well-grounded habit with me, and tends
> to be left to one side in the rush of so many other things."

The letter closes with a characteristic reference to my music—Bob Miller never forgot that it was my first love. "How is your piano playing these days? And have you been writing any more music for the sea now that you have really experienced her?"

I didn't hear from him again until the end of November 1950. By that time, he was having to contemplate returning to Canada. He had hoped, he said, to remain at Bad Boll until August of 1951, but "the pressure is on me to come home in June when my brother is thinking of getting married . . . I have resolutely (I hope) put to one side all temptations to stay away any longer."

Yet the prospects of coming home were by no means without their shadow side. "I am much puzzled when I think about coming home, what I should do, etc." I'm sure it never occurred to him to take up any work that he could not consider Christian ministry; but 'The ministry' in the usual sense—parish ministry—no longer appealed to him, I think. "I have become somewhat afraid of the church 'ghetto,' which has made the church here in Europe so incapable of doing its job, and so little able to free itself from its trammels even when it begins to realize its situation."

> There have to be much more radical experiments in the life
> of the church than there have yet been. Some of us have
> to get onto the frontier, where there are no beaten paths
> of how and what to do . . . and I don't mean the somewhat
> romantic conception of frontier that we have from our Ca-
> nadian history. The 'other' world of the working man that
> has grown up here in Europe is completely isolated from
> the church, and the latter is so unrealistic. God will have us
> where the people are, with them in their life and work, even
> when they don't understand, rather than waiting for them
> to come to us, or going around in our own little circles. He
> who loses his life . . . goes for the church first and foremost,
> but like everything else in this world she has become very
> good at holding on to it. I see things much clearer here than

I do at home. That comes of course from being away for
so long, and having worked myself into the situation here.
But also I think the problem is much further along here,
and because the situation is so much more desperate it is
also much clearer. I sometimes wonder, having seen and
understood all that, if there is not a responsibility to stay.
The need for and possibility of such radical experiments are
much greater here.

Reflections such as these should be kept carefully in mind by
any who want to understand the course of Bob Miller's life during
the decade that followed. Like some others among the brightest
and best of those who found their way into the ministry of mainstream Protestant denominations in the 1940s and '50s, the vocational question for Robert Miller at this point was not whether
the Christian faith could be sustained in our changing world, but
whether *the church* could ever again be the appropriate vehicle for
the gospel. To many, it seemed not only remote from the actual life
of the world but also forgetful of its own message—if it ever knew
it! This letter, the last that I received from Bob during his European sojourn, ends with a reference to Roman Catholicism—which,
quite clearly, the writer cannot regard as a serious alternative to
mainstream Protestant malaise (though, reading this paragraph,
one should remember that it will be ten years before Vatican II):

"I had the opportunity of taking three days along the Medi-
terranean coast a couple of weeks ago. It was wonderful to be in
this other world of perpetual sunshine, blue, blue water, and vivid
colourings, though we had hardly time to enjoy it properly because
we had to always be on our way to get back here in the appointed
time. The R.C. church is much more understandable in this world,
to which it seems to belong with all its tinsel. A good Dutch Calvinist or a Puritan Father would be just out of place in this world."

4

Before bringing this section of my biographic reflections to an end,
I should like to comment briefly on this initial stage in my long

friendship with Bob Miller. What has struck me most forcibly as, sixty years later, I reread and reviewed the letters that I received from him during his three-year sojourn in Europe (1948–1951) is the sheer fact of their existence. In the traditions both of Athens and Jerusalem (e.g., Aristotle and Jesus), the thirtieth year of life has been regarded as a, or perhaps *the*, crucial point of transition, the age of maturity. Bob Miller was not only passing through that personal 'paradigm shift' during the years 1948–1951, but he was also being subjected in a dramatic way to the turmoil that accompanied the last gasp of the Western age of idealism and the beginnings of what W. H. Auden called "the age of anxiety." In a manner that must surely apply to very few North Americans, Bob not only experienced the theological question-mark that was being written over the whole of liberal modernity (in the teachings of Karl Barth, particularly), but in Bad Boll he was thrust body and soul into the sociopsychological realities of that end-time—"the shaking of the foundations," as Tillich named it. Every one of Bob's letters to me at that time was written under duress: the strain of trying to find his way as a rather "innocent" Canadian among "a great and wise people," the strain of trying to comprehend another language, the strain of trying to communicate (in that "square-edged language," as Harvey Cox once called the German tongue!) with persons whose lives had been utterly shattered by events—and, beyond these, the ongoing strain of simply finding enough time to indulge in "luxuries" like writing letters. *And yet they were written*--and written to a young person nearly a decade younger and far less sophisticated than he, educationally speaking—someone with whom he had spent only a few hours during the summer of 1948. Again and again, as I read and reread these old letters from my youth, I was amazed at the sheer patience and seriousness with which their author approached his correspondence—his 'ministry to Douglas Hall,' if I may put it so. In none of the letters, even those which preceded my decision to enter the ministry, does he 'talk down' to me. Profound and difficult subjects like the nature of faith, the authority of Scripture, the quest for personal security, the relation between inferiority and superiority complexes, the mission of the church and its failure to speak to the contemporary condition of humanity: these and many other subjects that would come to occupy my thoughts during the eleven years of my university and seminary studies, and beyond, were already broached in these letters from the old flagship of Christendom. I can only assume that Bob Miller knew or suspected, even then, that what he was writing in these letters would have a deep and lasting influence on the course of my life. And of course it did—not by itself, to be sure, but as the initial impetus of a message that I was obviously needful of hearing and ready to hear.

A second generalization that I would like to make at this point is that my Beausoleil encounter with Bob Miller and the correspondence that resulted from that meeting established, for me, a lasting impression of the essential character of the one who first conveyed that message—"the messenger." The "message"—and for Christians that means the gospel—always transcends the messenger. The messenger, whether he or she is called Paul or Augustine or Luther or Theresa of Avila or Karl Barth or Barbara Brown Taylor or Bob Miller or Douglas Hall, always receives the message, if it is genuine, from beyond the possibilities and impossibilities of his own mind and psyche; it is never just *his* or *her* message, though it necessarily bears the imprint of a particular personality. For one thing, the messenger himself or herself always stands in need of hearing the message again and again—that too is an implicit and sometimes explicit presupposition of Bob's letters. The messenger is never wholly conformed to, or transformed by, the message. So there is no justification—*ever*—for any kind of idolatry, adulation, or whitewashing of the blemishes and faults of messengers. Protestants have always questioned, even, the no doubt humanly laudable practice of naming certain individuals saints. "We have this treasure in earthen vessels!"

But *gratitude* is never out of place, I think. And I am eternally grateful to the young Bob Miller for taking such trouble as he took to help me achieve something like a human and Christian maturity of my own. Beyond that, I am also convinced that the one who performed this great service for me (and for many others, too!) was and remained, essentially, the person whose generosity of spirit, depth of understanding, human warmth, and humor are revealed in these letters. I am moved to make this observation for a particular reason: *subsequently,* and especially in the middle and later years of his life, Bob Miller often struck people as being withdrawn, abrupt, detached and even uncaring. The unfortunate but perhaps inevitable conflict over the SCM Book Room, about which I shall say a little later on, had the effect, for some, of transmuting the pensive, private and critical-thinking side of Bob Miller into an aloof, reclusive or even somewhat misanthropic caricature of the man. It is true, I think, that the outgoing, articulate and compassionate aspect of the person revealed in these letters, as in the few days on sunny Beausoleil, became less transparent as the years went on. The times, as I shall try to show in part 4, introduced subtle changes by which even the most steadfast were affected. The *reticence* of the older Bob Miller cannot be denied. But I prefer to attribute this to Bob's unusual kind of consciousness, which certainly contained elements of irony and skepticism, but should not be confused with cynicism, disillusionment, or the capitulation to silence that is one of the great temptations of aging. In a recent letter, William Fennell, for many years professor of theology at Emmanuel College, wrote that he thought of Bob Miller, whom he knew quite well, as "a quiet Kierkegaardian—if that isn't a contradiction in terms."[4] I rather like that. SK too combined piety and irony in a unique and provocative and often puzzling manner. At the same time, I doubt that "the melancholy Dane" was capable of the kind of outbursts of humor that Bob Miller sometimes brought to his discourse with others. I cannot imagine Kierkegaard driving wildly through the countryside whilst singing Gershwin's "It Ain't Necessarily So!" at the top of his lungs!

My point just now however is that this Kierkegaardian streak in Bob Miller, or however it may be named, ought not to

4. Bill Fennell also wrote in the same letter that he had urged Victoria University to grant Bob Miller an honorary doctorate. This suggestion was not taken up by the board, however, because some of its members feared that such a gesture would be tantamount to siding with Bob in the dispute with the SCM leadership.

overshadow the sense of Christian discipleship that was as strong in Miller as in Kierkegaard himself. Both certainly knew the dark side, and both were destined to know it more intimately as they moved through life. Their testimonies to the light that "shines in the darkness" would have been poorer, and perhaps incredible, apart from that familiarity. But however the dialectic of light and dark may have swayed Bob Miller's life, I am convinced that the *persona* whom I encountered long ago on that island of the sun and in those early letters from him was permanently present in the ongoing life of this man, whatever its vicissitudes. In different language, I think that Bob was 'being himself' then in a way that was sometimes obscured later on, even if there was more to 'himself' than is or could be revealed in these early encounters. And of course there was.

2

The Book Steward

1

"KNOWING" ANOTHER HUMAN BEING is a matter far more complex than is usually assumed. Does one ever really *know* another? Don't our claims to *know* someone contain a good deal of presumption, if not even greater sins? *Really* to know someone surely must entail a certain awe and modesty in the face of life's mystery; for what, in the whole range of human experience, is more mysterious than the unique being of those one knows *best*?

In 1948 I began to know Bob Miller, but even the *factual* side of his life prior to that meeting has only come to me, in bits and pieces, over the six decades since that initial encounter, and I have still needed the help of three or four others to gather some of these facts. It is probably fitting, however, that at this juncture in my recollections I should share with the reader what I know of these.

Robert Whiteley Miller was born on June 10th, 1919, in the city of Toronto. His father, Henry Miller, was a salesman for a fabrics company in Toronto, and his mother, Gladys Whiteley, born in the Canadian West, had trained and worked as a milliner. Bob was their first child. Later a brother, Douglas, would enter the family circle. Doug. Miller, whom I met only once, also became, in time, a United Church minister. He predeceased his older brother by several years, and his death after a debilitating illness[1] was a great sorrow both to Bob and to their mother.

The family lived in Toronto's west end, as it was then, After Bob's return from Europe in 1951 he took me to their home on Windermere Avenue one morning. It was a comfortable and modestly furnished middle-class home, typical of that area; but I do not know whether it was the home into which the newborn little Miller was brought to begin his life. Henry Miller, as he is remembered by Bob's cousin, Mary McInroy, was a gentle, affable man. He and Mary's father, Murray McInroy, were first cousins and the two families often visited back and forth. Mary, who became a nursing instructor and was close to Bob, remembers that when Bob's father visited her in the Toronto General Hospital after an operation she had had, a nurse noticed that cousin Henry was crying after their visit. "He was such a pussy-cat!" writes Mary with obvious affection—and "this picture suggests such a difference between father and son, Bob being quiet, more reserved."[2]

Bob attended the Runnymeade Collegiate, the high school that was also attended by his friend John Coleman, later a distinguished professor of mathematics at Queen's University and husband of the late Marie-Jeanne de Haller, a Swiss Reformed Christian who was active in the World Student Christian Federation and well-known to Bob Miller and many other persons involved in the Canadian Student Christian Movement. John Coleman, who was a little older than Bob, says that he did not know Bob at high school, but only came to know him later— "We never discussed Runnymeade Collegiate to my knowledge. We certainly shared theological and political opinions. Over many years, with Marie-Jeanne, we shared a long correspondence . . . I was always

1. Mary McInroy writes: "Douglas . . . had limited ability to move without support. He resembled a multiple sclerosis victim." [Her letter of March-April 2010]. Paul Warner (email of May 12, 2010) specifies that Douglas Miller died at 105 Howland Avenue in Toronto of ALS (Amyotrophic Lateral Sclerosis or Lou Gehrig's Disease. Part of Bob's modest earnings went to the support of both his brother and his mother).

2. From a letter to me dated London, March-April 2010.

amused that his letters to us were always addressed to MJ, who loved him even more than I did."[3]

As I've indicated in the previous part of this paper, Bob Miller enrolled in an undergraduate program at Victoria College (now Victoria University) in the University of Toronto in 1940. Meg Young thinks that it may have been a course in the field of commerce and finance. I can only assume that he was a bright and engaged undergraduate, but I know that he was also a gifted sportsman who excelled in track and field especially, and was (he told me) being seriously considered, as well, as a tennis professional. Together with Margaret (Grant) Young, whom he met at this time, Bob was elected to the student council of 'Vic' in his first year, and was very popular among his peers. At least one young woman, according to Meg, fell deeply in love with him—not the last, nor probably even the first, of a series of romantic idylls that the handsome young man would inspire.[4]

More important, Meg told me that in their youth Bob and a cousin of his had fallen in love and wished to marry, but that (in her understanding of the matter) "the mothers" of the two were opposed to the prospect of their marrying. A later communication from Bob's close friend, Paul Warner, confirms this and adds some significant information about the relationship and its lasting consequences for Bob. "I don't know whether you were aware of Robert's relationship with his distant cousin, Vivian, who was in love with him when they were students at University. It was always a tragedy for him, as they were so close, and it affected him all of his life. [It also in some way accounts for] the distance that he kept from other women. He was able to resume a correspondence with her during the last years of his life."[5]

I do not know when Bob decided to enter the ministry of the United Church, nor am I cognizant of what influences brought about that decision. Meg told me that she didn't remember Bob's

3. E-mail message from John Coleman dated January 21, 2010.

4. Margaret (Grant) Young died on April 18, 2010, shortly after I spoke with her about this book. She was eighty-nine.

5. E-mail message from Paul Warner on April 30, 2010.

having discussed his interest in the ministry with her, though they were in frequent discussion; he simply announced it one day, she said. His family was not very active in the church, so far as Meg remembers, though Bob himself *may*, she thinks, have been somewhat involved with the Young Peoples' Union (YPU) of one of the United churches. He certainly came to know Ray McCleary during his undergraduate years, and while Meg does not think that Ray was anything like a "pattern" for Bob's decision to enter the ministry, she does know that he admired Ray's work.

Whether McCleary or someone else suggested to Bob that he study at Union Theological Seminary, is not known either; in any case, Union Seminary in 1943, when Bob first entered that community, was certainly one of the most—if not *the* most—talked-about institutions of Protestant theological education on the North American Continent. Reinhold Niebuhr, who in 1928 had gone to teach at Union from his well-established parish work in Detroit, had achieved a great name for himself well before the outbreak of World War II in the fall of 1939, and in fact in that very year, as the bombs were beginning to fall on Edinburgh Niebuhr was offering the second part of his famous Gifford Lectures in that city. These lectures were published under the title *The Nature and Destiny of Man*, in two volumes in 1941, just two years prior to Bob Miller's registration at Union. They established Niebuhr as a serious theologian who could give a luminous and comprehensive account of the Christian faith in our time, and not only a generalist or social ethicist. Bob once told me that he sat beside Niebuhr at a banquet during his first year at the seminary, and the guest on Niebuhr's other side began speaking with enthusiasm about Niebuhr's books. Dr Niebuhr asked her which of his books she had most appreciated. When she answered *Leaves from the Notebook of a Tamed Cynic* the Gifford Lecturer was somewhat taken aback: that book had been his first publication, and consisted of the reflections of "a callow young fool" (as he calls himself in its opening pages) on his life as a parish minister in Henry Ford's Detroit. The author's remonstrance notwithstanding, *Leaves* remains a favourite of many still.

It was chiefly due to Niebuhr's interest in and personal knowledge of the contemporary situation in his father's native Germany that Paul Tillich was brought to Union Seminary in 1934, the first non-Jewish intellectual to be dismissed from his professorship in Germany (Frankfurt) by the Nazi regime. I do not know whether Tillich made much of an impression on the twenty-four-year-old Miller; the evidence I have suggests that he did not, though in later years Bob carried Tillich's *The Courage to Be* among the stack of books he took with him on his visits to Canadian universities as SCM Study Secretary. Besides these two luminaries, the Union Seminary faculty in the 1940s and '50s boasted prominent scholars in all the major disciplines of Christian faith, and internationally known figures like Emil Brunner, Martin Buber, H. Richard Niebuhr, Arnold Toynbee, W. H. Auden, T. S. Eliot, M. M. Thomas, M. C. D'Arcy, and many others were regular visitors and lecturers there. As Tillich once put it, "If New York City is the bridge upon which international traffic enters North America, Union Seminary is the lane of that bridge upon which theological traffic travels."

These teachers were all bound to have an impact on the young Canadian, and I was told (by Ray McCleary) that he was again very well thought of among his fellow students at Union. John Coleman Bennett, who in the mid-1950s became my own *Doktorvater* and was later named president of the seminary, remembered Bob well, as did John's perspicacious and politically outspoken wife, Anne. But perhaps the most influential person in Bob's sojourn at Union Seminary was his fellow student, Ellen Flesseman-van Leer. For this reason I will devote a separate section of this chapter to their relationship.

2

A story circulated among a few of Bob Miller's friends to the effect that after encountering Ellen Flesseman in some of his classes, Bob determined to ask her for "a date"—only to discover that she was already married.[6] Whether the story is truth or fiction I do

6. An alternative account of their meeting is provided by Evelyn Reid,

not know; but it is at least symbolically true in that it establishes the fact that this was, for both parties, a relationship of depth and endurance. From 1943, when Bob began classes at Union Seminary, until Ellen's death in 1991, the two were very close friends. Ellen was frequently in Canada and, as we have already seen in connection with his European studies and work, Bob Miller was quite often in Holland. Most of Bob's friends knew Ellen as well. I myself was with her on several occasions—including one unforgettable journey in my VW Beetle from Kingston to Toronto, during which she asked if she could drive, and then scared me to death as she ignored completely the speed limits on our Canadian highways and drove as though she were on a speed-limitless German autobahn! Rhoda, my wife, while still Mission Secretary of the Canadian SCM, knew Ellen well and admired especially the compelling and provocative manner in which she conducted her famous Bible studies.

Ellen Flesseman-van Leer was seven years older than Bob Miller. By the time they met in New York City, Ellen had already lived a fascinating—and sometimes a dangerous—life. The following article is to be found on the Internet under her name. It has been translated into English by my Dutch colleague at McGill, Professor Gerbern S. Oegema:

Flesseman-van Leer, Ellen

Reformed theologian (Berlin July 17th, 1912 – Ermelo June 18th, 1991)

Her way to theology was long and full of curves. She originally wanted to study the Dutch language, but in the end chose

---

who, since she heard it from Bob himself, no doubt has the correct version: Ellen and Bob "were in a classroom at Union Seminary in New York. He in the row behind her. He introduced himself to her, and she did likewise. They discussed an upcoming lecture that night. Ellen said she would like to go, but had a young child and was not free to go. They discussed a baby sitter, and this drew to Bob's attention [his own uncertain financial situation], so he offered to watch the baby while Ellen went to the lecture, since he had already heard the speaker. This is how he first got to know Ellen. After that, Bob often baby-sat for her. (This amused me greatly at the time, because I could never visualize Bob as a babysitter.)" [E-mail of May 14, 2010]

Classical languages in order to become a teacher. Through her acquaintance with the NCSV,[7] Ellen Flesseman, who was raised in a secular Jewish milieu, began to read the Bible. In 1939 she was baptized. The war brought her to the USA, where she was for some time cashier in a circus. A course in Hebrew was her entry into the study of theology, which was interrupted by a ministerial appointment in [a desolate village in] Northern Ontario. In 1946 she continued with her studies of theology in Leiden, where she obtained her PhD in 1953.

Ellen van Leer was born in Berlin. Her father was a Jewish Dutchman, who was married to a German woman whom he had met during one of his business trips. The couple settled in Berlin, but moved shortly before the First World War to Bussum [Holland], where Ellen attended primary and secondary school (HBS). She did not finish the HBS, because the family moved to Amsterdam, where she then attended the gymnasium (Lyceum).

In 1930, she began to study Classics at the University of Amsterdam, completing her course after six years. She returned to her old gymnasium, but now as teacher. In 1938, she had to give up her job, after her marriage with lawyer Albert Flesseman, who was also Jewish. In the meantime, through a female friend, she had been in touch with the Netherlands Christian Students Association. She found the Bible a strange book, difficult to understand; but the quest for God would not leave her alone. A distant cousin in Berlin brought her into contact with the Confessing Church [*Bekennende Kirche* in Germany]. In 1939 she was baptized in the Dutch Reformed Church.

In May 1940, her husband fled to England to fight with the Allied Forces, leaving his wife and a daughter behind. As he was not accepted for draft in England, he continued to the USA, from which he was able to send a sign of life to his wife. Businessman Bernard van Leer, a brother of her father, organized a visa for her. Van Leer, who at the end of 1940 had sold his factories for a good price, with a lot of clever and courageous dealing, paid two million [guldens] for the visa. In exchange he was

---

7. Netherlands Christian Students Vereiniging [Association], i.e., the Dutch SCM.

allowed to travel to the USA together with his family as well as
Ellen Flesseman-van Leer. An SS officer accompanied them to
the Spanish border.

Via Portugal they reached the USA, where Ellen was re-
united with her husband. She started studying theology at the
New York Union Theological University [*sic*!], studying with
Paul Tillich and Reinhold Niebuhr, among others. In 1948 she
completed her studies in Leiden, where she did her Ph.D. five
years later under the supervision of Bakhuizen van den Brink;
her dissertation was entitled "Tradition and Scripture in the
Early Church" and was an effort to get a hermeneutical grip on
Biblical text that were especially difficult to interpret—which,
given her linguistic background was not a surprising choice for
Flesseman.

That the relation between Church and Synagogue was
her second major interest is also not surprising. In 1949, one
year after the establishment of the State of Israel, she spoke at a
council of Reformed ministers about Israel as "a sign of God's
faithfulness," also a sign of the lack of power on the part of European Christianity to protect the Jews during the 12 years of
Nazism, and finally a sign of hope that the Jewish people would
find their Messiah. Her special position as Jew and Christian,
sitting on two chairs, made her reject the divinity of Jesus. In
consequence she also distanced herself from the virgin birth
as well as the trinity. However, her faith in the resurrection of
Jesus remained unchanged and was a clear demarcation from
her Jewish faith.

Shortly before her death in 1991, Flesseman, who in the
seventies had visited the Palestinian refugee camps, revised her
opinion about Israel being a sign of God. Not the State of Israel
(she now felt) but the return of the Jewish people is a sign of
God—thus exchanging her 1949 statement, which was political, for a Biblical one.

Flesseman did not occupy any official Church position in
the Netherlands, nor did she ever have a university position.
According to theologian Hendrikus Berkhof, with whom she
was very close, this was because the institutions involved believed "that such a position could not be filled by a housewife"
For a long time, until 1972, when she became known through

her lay dogmatics, *Believing Today*, she was better known abroad than in the Netherlands. Her dissertation on [tradition and Scripture] had drawn more attention internationally than at home in the Netherlands; her work with the World Council of Churches was mostly unnoticed at home as well. Until late in her life, she preached in Amstelveen, where she lived, and worked as a 'freelancer.'

[Written by Peter Bak, for *Protestant.nl*, August 29th, 2008]

The "desolate village in Northern Ontario" where Ellen served as pastor of a United Church for about a year was Hornepayne. It is located half way between Toronto and Winnipeg, well north of the beaten trail, and is reputed to be the coldest spot in Ontario. I am sure that Bob Miller, who at the same time had gone to his Saskatchewan mission field, had something to do with Ellen's appointment in Hornepayne. She returned to the Netherlands in 1946. The conditions of the war and its chaotic aftermath would have prevented Ellen's earlier return to Holland.

Dr Flesseman-van Leer was a great admirer of Reinhold Niebuhr, and it was rumored about Union Seminary during my own student days there that Niebuhr himself claimed that the two students who had most profoundly affected his theological thought, both women, were Ellen Flesseman and his wife, Ursula Keppel-Compton, who came to Union Seminary as a graduate student from England the same year that the German Dietrich Bonhoeffer entered that seminary (1930). I can quite personally vouch for Ellen Flesseman's loyalty to Niebuhr. During a visit Ellen made to Union in 1956, I invited her to engage in informal discussion with a group of my fellow students in my room one night. Rather recklessly, another student and I, both avid Barthians at the time, compared and contrasted Reinhold Niebuhr with our then-hero, Barth. Next morning after chapel, Ellen purposely sought me out. She had something to say to me, and it cut to the quick: "I think you are *stupid!*" she barked at me. She would not have her beloved Niebuhr, with whom she was staying as guest, criticized by the likes of us. She was quite right!

Yet the fierceness of her message to me on that occasion (fortunately ameliorated by kindlier words on subsequent occasions)
is indicative of one of Ellen's character traits: though she was also
capable of considerable personal charm and of a lively sense of
humor, she possessed a ("typically Dutch," some would say) impatience with those who held what she thought were erroneous
("stupid!") points of view, and the outspokenness that usually ac-
companies such impatience. And I am sure that this quality in
her was rather enjoyed by Bob Miller, who, like many Canadians,
preferred straightforward honesty in others and deplored mere
("American"?) "niceness." But the bond between these two obviously transcended all such character-traits and satisfied in each
of them certain deeply human needs and longings. Prior to her
death in 1991, Bob Miller telephoned Ellen daily for a week or
more, and he went to Holland for Ellen's last three Christmases.
One can't help wondering whether, under other circumstances, the
two might have found marriage, a state which they both honoured,
a natural flowering of their close relationship, though in many respects they differed markedly from one another.

Theologically speaking, I think that Bob Miller was and remained more unambiguously ("orthodoxly") Christian than was
Ellen Flesseman who, with her Jewish background, had difficulty
(as we have seen) with the Trinitarian and christological aspects of
Christian orthodoxy. In a letter to me which I mentioned earlier,
the Canadian theologian William Fennell wrote of Ellen that she
"was a word-for-word disciple of Barth"; but Barth would certainly
not have accepted as authentic Christianity a creed that denied the
validity of the Trinity, the divinity of Christ, or even the virgin
birth. In this respect, at least the Miller of the letters I have quoted
in Part I was much more a "disciple" of Karl Barth than was Ellen. Whether in later life he would have endorsed his own earlier
views is a moot question, but he certainly did not change his mind
publicly or in my hearing. Of course, Bob Miller never pretended
to be a theologian or a biblical scholar, and Ellen Flesseman-van
Leer was both in a quite intentional and public (though never 'official') sense. For all that, I know that Bob greatly respected her

theological and ethical thought, and that he was particularly proud of her work on Christian-Jewish dialogue, and with the World Council of Churches. I remember how he whispered to me with obvious delight one day that "Ellen now moves in the highest theological circles of the World Council—with Gerhard Ebeling and others!"

3

As I have indicated in Part I, the death of his father in 1945 brought about Bob's decision to return to Toronto for the completion of his Bachelor of Divinity degree at Emmanuel College, the largest theological college (seminary) of our denomination. At that time, the most influential professor in the field of systematic theology was John Line. Professor Line had also taught in the fields of philosophy of religion and Christian ethics. He was an inspiring teacher and presence. He was still part of the Emmanuel faculty when I studied music at the Royal Conservatory in 1948–1949, and I was able to hear him, as well as one of his most promising students, a young woman, when they came to address the Young People's Union of WoodGreen United Church. As William Fennel attests, "I believe [Bob Miller] admired John Line, who gave him his basic theological start."[8] It will be pertinent to this account, then, to offer a brief synopsis of the *curriculum vitae* of this interesting (and alas almost forgotten) Canadian theologian. As even this short resume will indicate, Line's combination of serious theological enquiry and social activism is reflected in the approach of his student, Miller.

John Line was born in England in 1885, and he left school at the tender age of 13 to become an apprentice to a carpenter. Five years later, as a result of responding to an advertisement for missionaries in the 'new world,' John was made a 'Methodist Probationer' in Newfoundland. He was ordained to the ministry of the Methodist church, and in 1914 he registered as a student at Victoria College in Toronto, qualifying for university entrance on

8. Letter to me dated January 2010

the basis of his first term's work there, when he received numerous prizes and medals.

After completing his degree at Victoria College and doing further academic study at Wesleyan College in Montreal, Line taught for a decade at Mount Allison University, two years at Pine Hill Theological College, and ten years at Victoria College as Professor of the Philosophy and History of Religion The remainder of his academic career—twenty-four years, plus four years in semi-retirement—was spent at Emmanuel College as Professor of Systematic Theology and the Philosophy of Religion. In his retirement he served as assistant minister at St. Clair Avenue United Church and St. Matthew's United Church in Toronto. He died in December, 1970. Dr Line's contribution to the church was summarized in the 1971 Minutes of Toronto Conference of the United Church of Canada as follows:

> Although he was an effective preacher and author, and a beloved visitor and pastor, it was as a teacher that he made his greatest impact. For almost half a century he was instrumental in shaping the thought and faith of students and future ministers. His theology was strongly evangelical so that at least one student could say, "John Line led me to Christ"; yet he never lost sight of the necessary social implications of the Gospel. During the Depression he worked and preached on the street corners in downtown Toronto among the unemployed. Often he took his students with him. It was for his social ministry in the Depression that Pine Hill conferred on him the Doctor of Divinity degree. In the year before his death, when the Canadian Theological Society, representing both Protestant and Roman catholic churchmen, decided to recognize honourary members, the name of John Line was the first to be passed unanimously.

John Line did not write extensively. The bulk of his publications were essays, articles for the *United Church Observer* and other Canadian media, and denominational publications. Many of his titles, however, indicate a breadth of theological, biblical and ethical interest, and a keen awareness of the spirit of his times. I suppose that he would not have regarded himself as 'a Barthian,' but he obviously had a deep appreciation for Karl Barth, whose works began to appear in English in the 1930s, and he communicated this appreciation to students like Bob Miller, who also found in John Line's example of ministering among the economically marginalized and working people precisely the kind of Christianity that is expressed in Bob's letters to me from Europe.

4

After his return to Canada in the spring of 1951, Bob Miller tried to find a way of exercising just that kind of ministry in Canada. I went to Toronto to meet him early that summer. It was a little awkward. After all, we actually had been in each other's presence, physically, only for a few days during the summer of 1948, at Beausoleil; and although the correspondence of the three previous years had been frequent, and often very personal, neither of us could be expected to have that comfortable feeling that comes with long acquaintance and physical proximity. I remember that we walked across the city from Broadview to a restaurant near the centre of town, where we met the Reverend Douglas Reid, who had graduated from Emmanuel at the same time as Bob. Our walk took us through the innovative 'Regent Park' housing development, which was still in the building at that time. We muddled our way through various attempts at real conversation, but there were long pauses, and I realized how fragile was the bond between us. Since then, I have sometimes wondered, in fact, whether the "quiet Kierkegaardian," had not already begun to inhabit the spirit of my friend. Had something happened in Europe to change the storyteller and letter-writer whom I had thought I knew better?

Part of the explanation, as I realized some weeks later, was that (as his later letters from Bad Boll had warned) Bob Miller had returned to his Canadian hometown less than enthusiastically, and he still very uncertain about "the next step." I know that he had hoped to emulate in some way the priest-workers in France. I think he may even have interviewed for two or three factory jobs, but it was not difficult for the canny employers to see that the applicant was hardly a typical jobless working-man, and, given the fear of union agitation in nonunionized industries, Bob soon realized that he would have to look for alternatives. The same fear of union agitation was experienced later by members of the Student Christian Movement (SCM) who took up factory work during the summers as part of a work-camp experience—one of Miller's passions about which I shall say a little in what follows. Richard Allen, one of these work-campers, was actually fired; and Rhoda Palfrey, a Nova Scotian who participated in the 1955 work-camp housed in Bathurst United Church in Toronto (and who five years later became my wife), was taken aside by the well-meaning proprietor of a button factory in Toronto where she worked briefly and told that a bright young girl like herself ought really to try to "make something of herself": what was she doing in a place like this?

Bob Miller's appointment as National Study Secretary of the Canadian SCM came about in the fall of 1951. As we have noted earlier, Bob had not been active in the SCM. as an undergraduate in Toronto, though he had friends—like Meg Grant (Young)—who were much involved in the Movement. One of the subjects that I introduced to him in my letters to him in Europe was my own experience of the SCM at the University of Western Ontario. I began to participate in the Western unit towards the end of my first year (1949–50), and by my second year of undergraduate work I was deeply engrossed in the life of the SCM on the campus. In fact, it quickly became one of the major interests of my university life, so that by the time I graduated from the UWO in 1953 I was not only president of the local unit but an enthusiastic supporter of the whole concept. It was natural for me, therefore, to let this enthusiasm spill over into my letters to Bob, and in one of his responses he makes specific mention of his interest in what I had reported about the SCM. I like to think that my commendation of the Movement played some part in Bob's decision to turn to the SCM as a promising context for the kind of ministry he was looking for.

The sixties were not kind to the SCM any more than they were to a number of other organizations that shared with the SCM a strictly "voluntary" basis both of membership and of economic support. I shall elaborate on that claim later (in part 4), but for the moment I simply want to make the point that the milieu that Bob Miller entered in 1951 was quite different from that of the remnants of the Student Christian Movement today. There were significant units of the Movement in every Canadian university. Some were of course larger and more prominent than others, but all enjoyed a certain respect on university campuses. One or two of the units had a reputation for partisan political activism—the McGill unit especially was considered "pink" if not radically socialistic, but this was not the norm. Most units were marked by a moderate or liberal Christian outlook,[9] but one which welcomed non-Christians and

9. From its website and its publications, my impression of what remains of the SCM in Canada today is that it likes to consider itself an organization of "the Left," and conveys the idea that this has always been the character of the movement. This is a revisionist approach to the history of the Movement. It is true that most of us who were SCMers in the 1950s and earlier probably preferred a social-democratic approach to government and society—like many others, I came from a household of CCF (later NDP) supporters; but few would think of themselves as ideological socialists or Marxists. It was a *pragmatic* socialism that inspired us, and even the term "the Left," which originated with the French Revolution and which has come into prominence on this side of the Atlantic in later years, was not part of our vocabulary.

Certainly at Western and, I believe, in the great bulk of the universities across the country, the *Christian* identity and mission of the Movement was dominant—while being critical of Christian exclusivism, denominationalism, and dogmatism. It was an *ecumenical* Christianity—as would be expected of an organization closely associated with the World Student Christian Federation and the World Council of Churches. While some there always were who felt that the term *Christian* ought to be stricken from the name, by far most SCMers, including those who did not embrace explicit Christianity, were clear that the chief purpose of the movement was to inspire a critically thinking form of discourse about the claims of the Christian faith and its pertinence to the life of the world—particularly the world as represented in the university itself. It was never a proselytizing organization any more than it wanted to be a Christian ghetto. It considered that the life of a university student would be incomplete, and possibly stunted, if he or she were not encouraged, during these few years of relative detachment from the demands of everyday life, to contemplate *religious* as well as other kinds of questions. While the SCM of my experience was undoubtedly oriented towards a *social* form of faith, it neither neglected the concerns of *personal* ethics nor

nonreligious persons, including professed agnostics and atheists. In contrast to the more conservative and "evangelical" students drawn to the InterVarsity Christian Fellowship (IVCF), students associating with the Student Christian Movement were not asked to adhere to specific creedal statements. One's "membership" in the movement *was*, in effect, the extent of one's involvement in its various activities; there were therefore many levels and shades of "belonging." The stated object of the Movement, which in Canada dated from the year 1921, was to examine the claims of the Christian faith as they impacted on the life of the world, beginning with the 'world' of the university itself. The SCM regarded itself as neither a substitute for the church nor a Christian ghetto in the midst of the secular university. Its membership on the whole maintained a supportive attitude toward the Christian (i.e., prior to Vatican II, almost exclusively mainline Protestant) denominations, most of which not only approved of the Movement but considered it an arm of ecumenical Christianity and contributed in varying degrees of generosity to its finances. As for the university, the SCM was generally understood to be a benevolent presence on the campus, a "space," so to speak, where serious students could integrate their religious and academic pursuits and where those committed to a life of faith could enter into honest dialogue with the possibilities and problems of the contemporary world.

While the SCM was not, and did not expect to be, endorsed by its host universities, it nevertheless usually enjoyed the trust of university administrations and, as a nondenominational, ecumenical organization it had a considerable appeal to Christian

---

did it discourage students of a more pietistic, conservative, or generally "capitalist" bent from full participation in its programs. One didn't have to be a 'Protestant' to be an SCMer, but neither did one have to be a 'Socialist.' The Canadian SCM was in the best sense an *open* community of concern and inquiry in its earlier (1921–1960) expressions; and one of the factors that brought about its marginalization in the post-1960s, I believe, was its too-uncritical identification with what are regarded (often questionably!) as "Leftist" political and ethical concerns. It would not be incorrect to say that this Movement, which managed for decades to remain open to "difference" in spite of the temptation of some to make it more explicitly *religious,* jeopardized this openness after 1960 by embracing an exclusivist *political* color.

teachers, administrators, and staff of Canadian universities who wished to exercise a degree of Christian discipleship in their place of employment. That kind of motivation was given an opening especially through the existence, in each university context, of a senior advisory board of the SCM. These boards were not only a source of continuity in the Movement, many of their members having themselves been active as SCMers during their student days; they also provided intellectual, spiritual, and practical help in the maintenance of the student-run units. Often the senior advisory boards included members of the university who were prominent in their fields of expertise or held important offices on the campus. For instance, during my undergraduate days at the University of Western Ontario not only were the dean of arts and the registrar active members of this advisory body, but the board included as well several of the most recognized and popular professors of the university; so that students who were active in the program of the Movement in this way became well acquainted with some of their teachers and administrators. If the university is a community of teachers and students, as it was classically depicted, the SCM was a particular and often an exemplary expression of that ideal—and that is precisely how I, for one, experienced the Student Christian Movement. In the formal and informal discussions that occurred in and around the SCM, the "idea" of the university became, for me and for many others, a concrete reality.[10]

Most of the units of the Movement in Canadian universities were able to employ full- or part-time "secretaries," as they were named—though their work was chiefly not "secretarial" in the commonly understood sense. Most important, these persons, who were usually older or graduate students (a few of them ordained clergy) functioned as counselors and assistants in relation to the student executives and confidantes, or counselors for individual students who sought them out in their (usually unpretentious, small but homey) offices. They reported not only to the student executive but also to the senior advisory board, which in

10. One of the most studied books in SCM circles during the 1950s was Sir Walter Moberley's *The Crisis in the University* (London: SCM, 1949).

most cases raised their modest salaries. In my experience (and I think this was generally the case) these secretaries performed a very important role in Canadian universities prior to the advent of denominational chaplaincies. It was in fact a serious blow to the SCM when the major denominations in Canada began in the late 1950s appointing chaplains on the campuses; for this meant, among other things, that the financial support on which the Movement had been able to rely was now channelled to the denominational chaplaincies. It also tended to move the religious situation in universities back to pre-ecumenical standards.

The programs of the local SCM units were informed, generally, by certain central concerns of the epoch and of universities and Christian churches. The purpose of the university; religion and science; Christianity and Communism; personal (including sexual) ethics; economics and social justice; war and peace; human solidarity and national interests; ecumenism—such were the topics that were regularly aired in public lectures or lecture series, study groups, or conferences. Specific faith concerns, such as worship, Bible study, doctrinal issues, relations between various churches and religious groupings, and the like, were pursued more intensely by the central core of the unit, though always open to everyone. Since, as I have already noted, there was nothing like official "membership" in the Movement, all of these activities were available to anyone interested; hence the life of the local unit was characterized by a constant flux and coming and going.

An ongoing debate throughout the Movement concerned the extent to which the adjective *Christian* in its nomenclature was an accurate, or even a desirable, description of the character of the Movement. A minority felt that this represented a too-exclusive approach to the mission and purpose of such an organization, and sometimes it was proposed by individuals or small groups that *Christian* be dropped from the name. This attitude did not, however, become a dominant one, and the majority recognized that a non- or intradenominational and ecumenical Christianity did, in fact, constitute the historic and sociological basis of the Movement and was legitimate as such.

The Movement was represented at the national level by a secretariat located in Toronto and housed, characteristically, in *very* modest quarters. Four of the officers of the National SCM were constant: a general secretary, an associate general secretary, a study secretary, and a mission secretary. The architects of the Movement were keen from the outset that the secretariat must always include at least one woman, and since, in the fashion of the day, it seemed inevitable that the general secretary would likely be a man, it was established from the outset that the associate general secretary would be a woman.[11] There was also a small support staff, and a number of volunteers for specific tasks. Both the Study and the Missions secretaries travelled regularly throughout the country, each of them visiting all the university campuses at least once during an academic year. The Study Secretary was responsible for stimulating study within the local units; the mission secretary had the particular task of alerting students to the mission of the Movement, and of related denominational and other groups, throughout the world. Naturally, however, the work of these two "traveling" secretaries overlapped a good deal. These men and women became collectively, in effect, the primary agents of continuity in the national Movement throughout Canada and in relation to its sister organizations abroad. Together with the general and associate general secretaries, they represented the "face" of the Canadian SCM, not only to the university units throughout our immense country, but also to the organizations and groups throughout Canada with which the SCM had close relations and to which, especially in the cases of the denominations, it looked for material support. The Canadian SCM had ties with the student Movement throughout

11. The office of associate general secretary was held by several well-known persons in Canadian church history: Gertrude Rutherford, Jean (Mrs. J. D. H.) Hutchinson, Harriet Christie and Margaret Prang. "I believe," writes Professor Prang of her three predecessors (who all subsequently became principals of the United Church Training School), "that they were early feminists trying to find roles for women in the church, beyond bake sales and teaching Sunday School" (E-mail to me on May 19, 2010). It would appear that the office of associate general secretary eventually morphed into the mission secretariat, which was in fact always held by a woman.

the world through the World Student Christian Federation, with headquarters in Geneva. In this way, too, the Movement was closely linked with the World Council of Churches; in fact it has often been observed that most of the officers and leading lights of the World Council (WCC) during the period in question had been active participants in the SCM as students.

Over the years, the SCM in Canada benefited from the leadership of several outstanding national secretaries, and Bob Miller became one of the most renowned of these. As study secretary from 1951 until 1957, he appeared at regular intervals in all of the university campuses in Canada where the SCM had units—which meant, virtually, all our universities. These campus visits, which would usually last for three or four days, were planned for in advance (sometimes more and sometimes less efficiently!) by the student executives of the local units with the help of their part- or full-time secretary. Usually the visiting national secretary would be expected to meet with the senior advisory board and other local church and university-related organizations. Often he or she would be asked to conduct a study session with members of the local unit, address public gatherings, deliver sermons or addresses in the context of worship, inform the unit of national SCM undertakings, and meet with individuals who had specific interests. I know at first hand, not only from my own experience on the student executive at 'Western' but also from my wife, Rhoda Palfrey, who was national mission secretary of the Canadian SCM for three years (1954–1957), that these traveling officers of the Movement had to be prepared for surprises—sometimes amounting to unsettling shocks!—as they moved from one campus to the next. They always travelled in the cheapest possible way, which in those days meant by train; their lodgings varied from student dorms to the private homes of senior friends; they were rushed from one event to the next, often without any advance warning. Rhoda remembers one occasion when, arriving at Memorial University in St John's, Newfoundland, after a rather arduous journey by train and ferry, she was informed by the local planning committee that she had been booked, that very night, to give a public address on the

Christian understanding of miracles! While advance planning was usually rather better coordinated than this, these secretaries, most of them still young persons themselves and not yet established in their disciplines or special interests, had to possess unusual combinations of social skills, intellectual acumen and curiosity, and (especially!) flexibility. Most of them could draw upon unique personal experience of one kind and another: Rhoda, for example, had spent the previous three years in Japan as a teacher of English in a large school for girls founded by our denomination; so it was always possible for her, as national missions secretary, to introduce themes and topics arising from that experience. Naturally, some national secretaries over the years were less able to "improvise" than others, and I remember as a student president having to host at least one such person who, though very enjoyable company, had very little with which to challenge the more serious among the student membership of the unit, let alone command the attention and respect of advisory boards and senior friends. That sort of thing was, however, the exception, not the norm.

Bob Miller was an exception, too—but at the other end of the spectrum. As we have seen, he had extraordinary gifts to bring to his meetings with local SCM units. Not only had he studied Christian theology and related subjects at the graduate level for several years and in some of the West's most exciting centres of Christian scholarship, but he had travelled quite extensively both in North America and Europe. He knew from personal experience both the university and the church. His exposure to the vast social and political problems of postwar Europe had left him not only with a storehouse of knowledge rare among Canadians but also a number of pressing questions that, sooner or later, would have to be faced by Christians throughout the world. Far more than most teachers of religion, theology and related subjects in academic settings throughout Canada, he had acquired a lived relationship with both personal and literary sources in which many of the great issues that would occupy church and society over the next decades were already articulated with passion and acumen. He had studied with some of the most influential leaders of theological thought in the West: Reinhold Niebuhr, Paul Tillich, Karl Barth, Hendrik Kraemer, Oscar Cullmann, and many other Christian thinkers who dominated Protestant thought throughout the world and, in some cases, continue to do so to this day. Very few if any of the professors in the various theological colleges of mainstream Protestant denominations in Canada had had Miller's kind of exposure to the presence and teachings of these giants of the post-war era, though some may well have been better-versed in the details of their writings.

Bob visited our SCM unit at Western several times during the two final years of my four-year undergraduate work there (1951–1953). It was always a special occasion, for me, when he appeared on campus, because these visits supplemented the few personal meetings that we had during those years. His public appearances at these times always filled me with pride. Whether in sermons during worship services in local churches, or formal or informal addresses before the advisory board and my fellow-students, I observed once again the same kind of charisma that Bob had shown at Beausoleil. The senior advisors realized that they were in touch with someone who could hold his own in the academic world, and the students were charmed by his combination of incisive (and sometimes sharply critical) thought and an unusual willingness to listen to their own experiences and points of view. To boot, the Bob Miller of these campus gatherings was simply a lot of fun—and not only the official representative of 'the national office,' but a human being whose real and vulnerable humanity could be glimpsed even during a short visit to a campus.

During his final two visits to Western while I was there (I was living in the new Huron College buildings then), we talked about my own future plans. I had assumed, as a candidate for the ministry of the United Church, that I would go on to Emmanuel College in the University of Toronto following the completion of my undergraduate degree. Bob urged me to think more boldly. My academic record was such, he said, that I should apply to the best American seminaries—Union, Princeton, Yale (Harvard in those days didn't appeal to most of us who were looking for graduate work in theology). I did that, and to my astonishment I was accepted at all of them—with bursaries thrown in for good measure! But with Bob's last visit we agreed that Union Seminary would be the best choice. Indeed, Union at that time (1953) was probably at or near the zenith of its reputation as the most exciting centre for Protestant theological studies on this continent. Union Seminary too was altered by the spirit of the sixties, and for reasons not unlike those that changed the SCM in Canada; but the decade from 1950 to 1960 was particularly stimulating, not only for the seminary itself, but throughout the North American church. There were many international scholars and students at the seminary then, including a significant contingent of Canadians; and many of the theologians, biblical scholars, and ethicists (among them Walter Brueggemann, Phyllis Trible, M. M. Thomas, V. C. Samuel, Walter Wink, Beverley Harrison, and Frederick Buechner) who became the teachers and writers of the next three or four decades were present as graduate students during those years. While I had every reason to believe that Emmanuel College and other theological colleges in Canada were worthy institutions, and indeed assumed that my own destiny would take me eventually into that national milieu, I was thrilled about studying at Union Seminary at least during my basic three years of foundational studies. (I ended up staying for seven years, but that was not part of the original plan.) So once again Robert W. Miller had greatly influenced the course of my life.

5

On May 18, 1953, I was at home in Woodstock, Ontario, with my parents and my two youngest brothers—my other three siblings had all married young and were living nearby. A friend from university visited in the late afternoon and evening, and my father (with whom I had argued that morning) found him a very congenial conversation partner: they both enjoyed the macabre—Dracula and all that. It was in fact an exceptionally enjoyable evening, and we all went to bed around midnight feeling, I think, rather good about ourselves. My graduation from the University of Western Ontario in nearby London was to take place in about three weeks. I lay awake for some time thinking how fortunate I was: I had never dreamt that I could become a university graduate, let alone find myself accepted for graduate studies at a famous institution in New York City.

Suddenly there was a flurry of activity from the adjoining bedroom of my parents and I heard my father rush to the bathroom. He was having a bad bout of indigestion—or so he thought. But within minutes after his return to bed a cry of dismay from my mother alerted me to the gravity of the situation. I rushed into their bedroom and found my father unconscious—or worse. A frenzied call to the hospital brought the doctor on duty to our home, and he attempted to revive my father through an injection directly to the heart. But it was too late: Dad had suffered a massive coronary thrombosis. He was forty-five years of age.

The shock of sudden death is like no other experience in life. Well over half a century later John Darius Hall's death still marks the most dramatic, and in some ways the most *traumatic* event of our family history. We were, of course, greatly comforted at the time by the sympathy and practical compassion of many neighbours, relatives, and close friends. For me personally, none of those who shared our family sorrow were more truly comforting than the three United Church clergy, all by now good friends, whose names appeared in the opening pages of this little account (and it is for that reason that I am recounting this event): Ray Mc-Cleary, Arthur Young, and Bob Miller. To my immense surprise and undying gratitude, all three appeared at my father's large funeral in Woodstock. They had taken the train from Toronto that morning. I have no idea which of them initiated the journey—it could have been any one of the three; but it was an act of unforgettable solidarity for the twenty-five-year-old that I was then, and I have never forgotten it.

The great question, then, was of course whether I would be able, under the new and devastating circumstances, to go off to New York City in the fall to begin my studies at Union Seminary.

My unmarried brothers were still very young (nine and sixteen); there were virtually no savings; the house was still mortgaged; my mother, who had been a primary-school teacher until she married in 1927, initially felt that she would never find work at her age and after so long a break from the profession that she loved. The whole family was in a quandary, the like of which can only be appreciated by those who have had similar experiences.

And one of my friends *had* indeed had such an experience: Bob Miller, the death of whose father had occurred just when Bob was completing the second of his three-year Bachelor of Divinity course at Union less than a decade earlier. It was therefore an unimaginable gift when, a week or ten days after the funeral, Bob showed up in Woodstock again, and stayed with the family for two or three days.

In that setting, he was quite simply . . . a friend. He was also a *pastor*. Years later, Evelyn Reid told me that Bob Miller had appeared at her door in New York City a day or so after the death of her husband, Douglas Reid, on October 23, 1970. Bob, she said, had secured a room at the YMCA nearby and stayed with the family a week. "He was," said Evelyn, "simply the best pastor I have ever known." I could identify wholeheartedly with that conclusion. Bob didn't burden us with advice or well-meant counsel. He simply lived among us for those hours, played darts with my little brothers (who admired him), talked quietly with my mother and me, listened to our sorrows and our future-shock, shared our laughter. And when he left, we knew, each of us, that we could go on. My sixteen-year-old brother set his course for serious high-school and university study, with periods of hard work in between—and became one of the most adept and dedicated teachers of mathematics the Ontario Secondary School System has ever employed. My nine-year-old brother, a little hellion in his childhood, settled down in a way that surprised us all—and in the end became a Christian minister himself. My mother, only forty-seven at the time, *did* return to teaching, found that she still loved that calling very deeply, and that she was good at it. She retired with a good deal of regret some twenty years later. And I, who in a mood of mixed guilt and elder-brotherhood had been ready to forego further pursuit of my vocation for the sake of supporting my bereft family, found the courage to watch my mother leave one morning, her books under her arm, ready to begin again, and myself to leave, a little later, to start my life in the big, totally unfamiliar city of New York—where, unknown at the time of course, I would remain for seven long years.

I certainly do not wish to suggest that all that "resolution" of the family impasse in 1953 was the consequences of Bob Miller's appearance at our modest home on Ingersoll Avenue. Of course not! Many others contributed to our healing, and many very practical and difficult challenges had to be met by each of us. But I know very well that Bob's visit with us brought a certain sense of calm and resolve to every one of us who were still at home; and, more important, I know that Bob Miller could never be portrayed *accurately* if this pastoral dimension of his persona were not given a prominent place. I—and we—have experienced it very often since, but at no time more dramatically than during this extremely unsettling moment in our family history, when we might all have gone in different ways had we not known the presence and the compassion of this good man and a few others of his brand of *Menschlichkeit*.

6

Over the next seven years, my visits with Bob Miller were sporadic. He was busy being study secretary of the Canadian SCM, and I was preoccupied with exciting theological studies which drew me more and more toward an academic career, though I never abandoned the thought that such a career would *of course* require some years in ordinary parish ministry. During the summers and at Christmastimes I spent as much time as possible with my family in Woodstock, and usually on these occasions there were brief trips to Toronto or some other occasion that would include short visits with Bob; but since I had not only to fulfil my 'mission field' obligations for the denomination but also make enough money to finance another year in 'the Big Apple' (as New York has since been called), there were all too few occasions during which to renew my acquaintance with my old friend and mentor.

I always knew, however, what was transpiring in his life, at least in a general way; and through letters, notes and occasional visits I kept in fairly close touch with him. Over the years, I saw him frequently enough in his Toronto offices to form a picture of what his daily life might be like. At various times I met most of the people with whom he worked: Ted Nichols,[12] the competent and genial general secretary; Nancy Dunlop, the office secretary; Laura Pelton, though not an employee of the SCM, was often present, and I learned with sadness of her death through cancer. I came to know Roy DeMarsh, Ted Nichols's successor as general secretary, very well. At that time I did not know Hilda Benson Powicke, who was mission secretary from 1948, but she became a household name after I married one of her successors. Other familiar figures of the period were Sheila McDonough (later a professor at Concordia University with expertise in Islamic studies), her brother Bart McDonough, Rose Komlodi (later, Mrs. Emil Fackenheim), Elaine Sinclaire and Evelyn Reid; and sometimes during the mid-fifties I probably first brushed shoulders, all unawares, with my future wife, Rhoda Palfrey, who from 1954 to 1957 was national mission secretary and thus came to know Bob Miller quite independently of me.

From time to time, Bob wrote to alert me to the names of students he had met in his travels who intended to study at Union: Robert Wright was one of these, as was George Mossman. In his letters there were always passing references to his work, and I marvelled at the number and extent of his trips across the country and beyond. In August of 1954 he attended the assembly of the World Council of Churches at Evanston and wrote, "I spent an evening

---

12. Ted Nichols died in 1974 at the young age of fifty-eight. He had managed through his skilful leadership and diplomacy to put the SCM of Canada on a fairly solid financial footing—or so it seemed until the main Christian denominations withdrew much of their support in their determination to establish denominational chaplaincies on the campuses of the country.

with Eric Hutchison, whom I had known in Geneva." Eric had been a senior student at Union when I arrived there the year before, and later he became a protégé and assistant of Bishop Stephen Neill, the great Anglican ecumenist. During that same summer Bob had "spent a week in each of the four work camps."

The Study Conference and National Council of the SCM was being held at Five Oaks that fall, and since that training centre of our denomination was near Woodstock, I took up Bob's invitation to spend a few hours with him there in September before returning to New York. This glimpse of Bob Miller "at work" remains in my memory as a rather frustrating visit. I had hoped to chat with him about my studies and experiences at Union, but he was so constantly engaged in conversation with others who sought him out that I had little if any chance to speak with him. The situation was rather more satisfactory in this respect at Christmas time. It happened that the first major gathering of what became the Canadian Theological Students' Conference was being held at Huron College in the University of Western Ontario—my alma mater; so of course I made the short trip up to London from my home in Woodstock, and spent a day or two at the conference, chiefly because of Bob Miller's presence there.

Few, I suspect, of the students who attended the fifty-sixth annual Canadian Theological Students' Conference meeting in Halifax in May of last year (2010) will have realized that this organization, which has become an important annual occasion for students of theology in both Protestant and Catholic churches, was the creation of the study secretary of the Canadian SCM. I believe there had been a kind of preliminary or organizational meeting in Winnipeg the year before, but the meeting at Huron during the Christmas break of 1954 was the first major gathering. As he moved back and forth across the country from 1951 onwards, Bob Miller recognized that the theological students of the various denominations in Canada were in need of a forum through which the growing ecumenicity of the Christian movement could find expression among those who were preparing for ministry. This first official meeting of the organization was a considerable success, and received a good deal of notice in the secular press as well as in church circles. In fact, a rather humorous incident occurred when the reporter from the *London Free Press* who came to interview some of those involved in the conference turned out to be an old friend of mine from our undergraduate days as naval cadets; and when it came time for pictures my journalist friend insisted that I should be the central figure, with Bob Miller and the main speaker for the occasion grouped around me—although I was not even an official delegate to the conference.

The keynote speaker at that first meeting of the organization was a rather impressive figure in Canadian religious and educational history: James S. Thompson, a Scottish Canadian philosopher of religion and United Church clergyman who had been the president of the University of Saskatchewan and also served for several years as the dean of the Faculty of Divinity (as it was then called) at McGill University. His subject was Søren Kierkegaard, and there are those who would say, I think, that "Jamie Thompson" was a spirit so unlike the melancholy Dane that he could hardly represent him with any credible witness! I remember that some of us, following the evening session of the conference one night, were invited to meet informally for a fireside conversation with the speaker in one of the elegant homes of a friend of Huron College. Dr Thompson at one point had occasion to refer to Kierkegaardian "inwardness" and in support of this referred to the oft-quoted remark of Jesus in Luke 17:21: "Behold, the kingdom of God is within you." Having just learned from John Knox or Fredrick Grant, my New Testament teachers at Union, that the King James Bible's translation of this verse was faulty (it should be "the kingdom of God is *in your midst*"), I, seated on the floor inconspicuously among my betters, could not resist, but blurted out, "Of course that's a bad translation." There was dead silence—until the brilliant but puckish Bill Coleman, principal of Huron, giggled; and then Dr Thompson continued his monologue without a comment. I suspect that "the quiet Kierkegaardian" was in silent agreement with the laughter of his friend Coleman, but as the organizer and major domo of the event, Bob Miller maintained a perfectly straight face, and perhaps he didn't approve of my sophomoric smartness—in which case he'd have been entirely in the right.

The annual Canadian Theological Students' Conference has served the students and seminaries of Canada for more than five decades, and after the Second Vatican Council it became as influential in Catholic as in mainstream Protestant circles of theological education. The twenty-fifth such conference was held in Montreal, and in a little ceremony at McGill University's Faculty of Religious Studies, I am glad to say, we finally acknowledged its founder formally. Richard Allen, history professor at MacMaster University and later Minister of Colleges and Universities in the Ontario NDP government of Bob Rae, expressed the gratitude of all for whom this annual gathering had been a major factor in the drawing together of Canadian Christians:

> I want to say how much I appreciate the opportunity of introducing the founder of the Canadian Theological Student's Conference to you on this occasion of its twenty-fifth anniversary. He is a man worth knowing. I first met him when he returned in 1951 from several very interesting years in Europe, where he had gone on a travelling scholarship shortly after the second world war. He studied under Karl Barth at Basel, knew Hendrik Kraemer at the Ecumenical Institute, and worked for a short time for the Evangelical Academies through which the German churches were attempting to lay new spiritual and moral foundations for post-war Germany. During that time he became keenly interested in post-war German literature and in modern art.
>
> Bob returned to Canada in 1951 when post-war enthusiasm for a new world order under the banner of the United Nations was dissipating with the onset of the cold war, when Canadian theology was walking uncertainly in the last phases of theological liberalism and the social gospel. The Student Christian Movement had just emerged from depression radicalism but was still a potent force in most universities. Into this milieu Bob came as a fresh voice, alerting our ears to a range of thinking as exciting as it was new to us . . .

> It was in these years of the mid-1950's that he saw the need
> to lift Canadian theological colleges out of an endemic parochi-
> alism, and founded the Canadian Theological Students' Con-
> ference towards that end.[13]

7

Mention has already been made, *en passant*, of the work camps
organized by the Student Christian Movement under Bob Miller's tenure as Study Secretary. The work-camp concept of course
predates its Canadian history. While Bob Miller was not its first
advocate in the Canadian context, he was, as Richard Allen notes,
"an enthusiastic promoter and leader [of the program] once he
returned to Canada to become Study Secretary of the S.C.M." I
would attribute Bob's promotion of the work camps to the kind
of thinking to which he had been subjected both at Union Seminary and at Emmanuel College, particularly in the person of John
Line. He had hoped to emulate some aspect of the French 'worker
priests' experiments, as I've noted earlier; but while that appeared
not to 'fit' the Canadian milieu in terms of his personal vocation, it
could, he believed, be implemented in another form through student work camps. The first one in Canada was held in Brantford
in 1948, and was led by the New Zealand writer and activist Alexander Miller. Again, Dick Allen's commentary is helpful on the
question of the background of the idea:

> There were work camps of one sort of another all over Europe
> in the post-war period doing reconstruction. There was also
> a strong work and worship tradition in which, in Canada and
> the S.C.M. Eunice Pyfrom was the leading figure. Some of that
> came out of the British S.C.M. and the Iona tradition. I don't
> think Lex Miller was the prime mover, but he certainly was
> an inspiration and led the first industrial work camp at Brant-
> ford in 1948 and the more notable one in 1949 in Montreal

13. From a typescript copy of Professor Allen's speech in the Junior
Common Room of the Birks Building, McGill University, dated February
1979.

(not more notable because I attended it, but by the presence of Dan—then Don—Heap, Bruce Mutch, Vince Goring and others. Lex must have had an earlier connection with the British S.C.M. because it published his *Christian Significance of Karl Marx*, which was already in circulation.[14]

The purpose of the work camps, at least one of which Bob himself led, stated in the most general terms, was to acquaint young people who were pursuing studies in various disciplines with the realities of life among those who must earn their livings in the often thankless and boring world of manual labour, to the end that at least *some* of those who could influence social and economic policy today and tomorrow would be better able to appreciate the struggles of the "working classes" and represent these in the public forum *with a view to change*. Students seeking admission to a work camp would be told in advance of what was expected of them. They would live together in relatively small groups, usually in church basements or other inexpensively acquired quarters. They would be expected, shortly after their arrival at the camp, to look for work in some factory or other outlet. They would pool their wages, and when the living expenses of the camp had been calculated at the end of the summer, would draw from the common fund what they needed, as individuals, to meet their economic obligations for the ensuing academic year (though some, by prior agreement, opted to keep for themselves the money they had earned, minus their living expenses). Three or more nights weekly would be spent in biblical and other types of study and discussion, and throughout the period a deliberate attempt would be made by all concerned to understand the dynamics of community life and to foster the building of genuine communality, understood in Christian or other humanitarian terms.

Anyone who has attempted to live in close proximity to others for a significant period of time will realize that such a life is by no means easy or problem-less. For young people reared in typically middle-class homes, having to share all the responsibilities of communal life can itself prove daunting. Once, during this

14. E-mail communication to me on March 4, 2010.

period, Bob Miller asked me if I would be willing to undertake the direction of such a camp: "How would you like to work in a factory and direct a work project this summer? It would take all your time from as early as you could begin till the end of August, and would certainly not be a rest."[15] I declined, as later I also declined Bob's offer of becoming an SCM campus secretary. I did so, not because I found the work too onerous, but because I had by then set my sights on graduate studies and a career in academic theology. I had had a fair share of life in the work-a-day world, and felt that I ought to vary my experience as widely as possible during my postgraduate studies. From the testimonies of others, however, and notably that of my wife, who was a member of the work-camp at Bathurst Street United Church during the summer of 1955, I know perfectly well that I should have had considerable difficulty adjusting my rather too assertive self to the rigours of group living, though I know that work in industry among 'ordinary' labouring people would not have troubled me greatly—it was, after all, my own domestic background. In any case, it is obvious that such work-camps—several of them operating simultaneously through a summer—could not have succeeded without patient and consistent leadership; and Bob Miller provided that leadership at the level of the national Movement.

8

It was not very obvious to me during the two years (1951–1953) that, as an undergraduate, I encountered Bob Miller as Study Secretary of the SCM, but I think that as Bob found his way into that work he gradually understood that his function among Canadian university students necessarily involved the transmission of knowledge and concerns that transcended the preoccupations of academic communities in our scattered and often rather parochial settings. Even before his three-year sojourn in Britain and Europe, he had been exposed at Union Seminary and elsewhere to theological and other ideas and literature that were still unfamiliar to

15. Letter of February 25, 1957.

most Canadian university or seminary communities. The works of Barth, dating from the second decade of the twentieth century, had been in translation for more than a decade by the time Bob Miller began his ministry, as had the books of the Niebuhr brothers, Paul Tillich, Rudolf Bultmann, and many others; but they filtered down into the colleges and seminaries very slowly. When Arthur Young sent me a copy of the first translation of Dietrich Bonhoeffer's *The Cost of Discipleship* in the summer of 1949, only a handful of reading Christians in Canada had heard the name of this now most renowned martyr of the twentieth century. The most "liberal" denominations in Canada were still under the sway of either the social gospel or the more personalistic or pietistic forms of nineteenth-century liberalism. Bob Miller was among the first intellectuals in Canada to have read the works of the scholar who, during the remainder of the century and beyond, would dominate the Protestant theological scene in the West.

In Europe, as we have seen, this familiarity with 'the new theology' was greatly enhanced for Bob by his studies with some of the very writers of these books; and, beyond that, he began to be conscious of other, secular literature that had become, and must become even more explicitly, the dialogue partner of any Christian who expected to understand the nature of the "world" that had come to be in the wake of two devastating world wars and the failure of Christendom. Existentialism was for Bob, as for many, the most articulate core of that new world view, and among the existentialists one name stood out, even though many would say that that name—Albert Camus—does not really belong among the existentialists. Even in his eighties, Bob Miller still marveled at the life of this extraordinary French thinker. On a visit with him in Victoria in the late 1990s, to which I'll refer again in part 4, Bob spoke almost with awe of his recent reading of the newly published "final work" of Camus, an incomplete autobiography in which the great author of *The Outsider* describes his "fatherless" childhood in Algeria, and the lifelong difference that was made for him by a humble but wise schoolteacher who made the young boy conscious of his human possibilities.[16] "Imagine," Bob exclaimed, "what might never have happened without the quiet work of that teacher!" Yes: where would any of us be without . . . messengers?

The SCM study secretary soon realized that works by such authors as these, and the graphic art that went with them, were still for the most part strangers to the Canadian young whom he encountered in his travels back and forth across our immense terrain; and thus it was that his suitcases became heavier and heavier. All those who remember him in this role from about 1954 onwards picture him, not only as an interesting and likable visitor from Toronto's "head office," but as the bearer of books and art prints that, in many cases, changed their worldviews. One of those young Canadian students, Robert Wright, wrote to me after Bob's death, as follows: "I also have many really great memories of Bob, particularly when he used to come to Alberta with his big suitcases of books—which later became the SCM book room, literally one room in the SCM house in Toronto. It was he who really encouraged me to go to Union—or at least calmly assured me that I shouldn't assume I wouldn't be able to go."[17]

The SCM Book Room in the beginning *was*, as Robert rightly says, Bob Miller's suitcase; and what made it an *extraordinary* suitcase was not just that it was filled with books but that the books with which it was filled were books *known intimately to its bearer!* The world is full of books. As Koheleth laments, there is no end to the writing of them! But the world is *not* filled with human beings who *know* many books, and can talk about them intelligently with those who do not. The SCM Book Store, whether in a suitcase or in several rooms in downtown Toronto (as it came to be) or in the late lamented Rochdale College, had this enormous advantage over almost every other bookstore of one's experience: its main 'Steward,' and those whom he trained, actually knew the books they sold! But this exception pertained only so long as that

16. Albert Camus, *The First Man* (trans. David Hapgood; New York: Knopf, 1995).

17. Robert Wright, writing to me on January 31, 2004, from rural Alberta after the death of Bob Miller.

man humbly self-described as 'Book Steward' was at his work; for knowing books is nearly as complicated as knowing people: it requires a lot more than just reading the books, or some parts of them! It certainly doesn't come from reading only book-*reviews* or publishers' catalogues. It is not for nothing that the CBC, for a period, commissioned Bob Miller to talk about some key books of the period on the air.

Many times between 1953 and 1960, I urged Bob to come to New York for a visit—after all, by 1956 I was a graduate student and tutor in his old *alma mater*; but until a certain event of which I shall speak later Bob always found it impossible to "get away." I knew that he really loved the big city, and would have been glad to experience Union Seminary in its most 'successful' phase, the 1950s; but his work always came first, and by 1957, when he gave up the often demanding and draining work with students on Canada's scattered campuses and became Book Steward (an office he himself created with the blessing of the Movement), his duties became even more exacting. By May 25th of that year, in declining yet another invitation to come down to New York, he wrote—

> I am in process of taking over the book operations, and do not have things organized so that someone else can look after things yet. Besides, it is the end of the month, when accounts have to be made up. I am planning late this year to make a trip to New York. I realize I have talked about doing so before without doing it. However, I shall not be travelling [as Study Secretary] any more, and will be better able to do such things. Also, I want to visit some of the book places down there . . .
>
> We are going to incorporate the business, and have received some investment capital from friends. *This is necessary to relieve the SCM from carrying the thing alone and using up all its spare cash in book investments.* We have a stock of close to ten thousand dollars, and for us that is not peanuts. If you know anyone with spare cash who would be interested in assisting such a venture as well as making a good investment (under very capable management!!) just tip them off. [*My italics*]

> Hope things go okay at the convocation, and congratulations on the S.T.M. I am impressed, even if you are not.[18]

A few months later, the wonder was still growing: "We have finished moving and painting and re-shelving books and are doing a booming book business, all of which is good but has made life hectic . . ."[19] And so it continued, year after year, until May of 1960, when, finally, Bob Miller's presence in New York City was urgently required!

9

The academic year 1959–1960 was a busy one for me. I was in the midst of my doctoral work at Union Seminary, and at least a third of my time was spent as tutor (teaching assistant) for three of my favourite professors—Paul Scherer, considered by many the greatest contemporary American preacher and teacher of homiletics; John Coleman Bennett, professor of systematic theology and then dean of the faculty; and J. Christian Beker, professor of New Testament at Union and, later, Princeton. In late January, Dr Harold Vaughan, secretary for colleges and students of the United Church of Canada, called a meeting of all Canadians currently studying at Union. There were some twenty-five of us, I think. Only one young *woman* appeared at the gathering: Miss Rhoda Catherine Palfrey, who, after three years as national mission secretary of the SCM and two as part-time secretary of the SCM unit at Dalhousie University, had decided the she really *had* to acquire a more mature knowledge of the faith and of the world, and had registered in the joint Union Seminary and Columbia University master's degree program on the history of Western thought. Dr Vaughan's meeting was the first occasion on which I had noticed Ms. Palfrey, and I dared, a few days later, to invite her to a concert of the Moscow Symphony Orchestra at Madison Square Garden, featuring the newly crowned winner of the Tchaikovsky piano competition, the

18. Letter to me of May 25, 1957.
19. Note of fall 1957, undated.

Texan Van Cliburn. The concert was on February 14th—only later did we realize that it was St. Valentine's Day!

We were old enough, and lonely enough, to recognize true love when it happened; so we did not waste time with the usual cat-and-mouse games of courtship. We married three months after that first date. We had so many things in common, though we were from different parts of our big country, and shared so many associations and friends—including the United Church and the SCM—that we felt we had known each other for a very long time.

It was obvious to us from the start that Bob Miller should preach the sermon at our wedding. Bob's response was immediate. A telegram from him dated March 29, 1960, reads: "Tried phoning all evening. Should have known you would be in the library! [an obviously ironic allusion]. Finally something exciting to bring me to New York. Glad Rhoda went to stimulate your imagination. Some philosophy she pursued. Bob"

A later letter remarked, "It seems quite natural now to think of the two of you together—I should have thought of it long ago!" Another note joked that the only unfortunate part of our invitation was that he would have to preach at our wedding; but then he added, "I think I'd have been a little let down if I hadn't been asked." Apropos his knowledge of the character and practices of Herr Professor Doctor Oscar Cullmann, he asked, "Should I wear my medals?"

The wedding took place in Christ Chapel of the Riverside Church on May 28th, 1960. Professor Paul Scherer officiated, attired in his wonderful Lutheran vestments, and many of my teachers of the past seven years were present, as well as American, Canadian, and other friends and members of our families. Rhoda and I sat for the sermon. Afterwards my elderly, Smith College–educated adopted aunt from New Jersey, Mary A. Kilborne, said of Bob Miller as he stood in his black suit and clerical collar in the pulpit of the chapel of the famous Rockefeller-built church, "Like a young Peter Abelard!"

His sermon—which he may have used on other occasions, for he, like the bachelor Dietrich Bonhoeffer, preached at the weddings of a number of his friends—was very moving, at least for us two (though I am sure Professor Scherer would have asked for a little more visible structure!). He drew on several biblical texts having to do with love—John 3:16, of course, but also Ephesians 3. He spoke quite directly to Rhoda and me, and as one who knew us well. But his sermon was in essence a theological commentary on the nature of love in Christian understanding.

> Love: fullness of being. . .patient and kind; modest, humble. Such is the nature of Him we know and acknowledge in the Church . . . That is really all we have to say about Him. That is really what we dare to say about Him. This is the way He is. This is the way He has acted in creating the world. This is the way he related himself to it and to his children. This is the source, the sustenance, the meaning, the end of human existence. This the way that we are bidden and given to live—*and occasionally do*.
>
> To say God is love does not mean love is God. Love is the way of God but it is nourished and sustained, given and re-stored by Him. Love is the way of our life in response to Him and to those with whom we are given to live.
>
> Love is existing and troubling, joyful but awesome. Noth-ing so moves and transforms us, so disturbs and frustrates us. This is the root of our sorrow and of our joy because it is the very root of our being. It is the nature we have been given and it is the very nature of Him who has given it to us. In this we come closest to ourselves, to each other, and to Him.
>
> In love we are exposed, attacked, become vulnerable. Through love we are laid open to the yearning and hoping, to pain and joy; the misery and triumph of human being pours in upon us and shakes the fragile walls of self-protection which we have built. We both desire and fear its devastation. Love casts us from the shore of self in which we try to haven our life, and involves us with another—with another self-protecting, self-grounding being . . .
>
> With the other, you begin to fashion your life anew—to-gether. You become a creature in love, a being in relationship. Your life is taken from you and is restored to you.
>
> Love replaces loneliness. You are now <u>with</u> another. There is now, always, alongside your life the other life. You take this

other life along with you wherever you go and with whomsoever you go, whatever you do . . .

There may be times when the fear—even the conviction—
of loneliness will return to you, even deepened because you
have been with another. Do not indulge yourself, but just there
reach out to one who is with you. And when you see the other
one turning back into his [or her] loneliness, follow after as far
as you can and there wait until he [she] discovers that you are
still with him [her] and that his loneliness is an illusion . . . [20]

You are now not only <u>with</u> one another; you now live—in
love—<u>for</u> one another . . . It is through you and with you that
the other is allowed to realise something of the fullness of his
own nature which he could never achieve alone. You must let
this fullness of the other have its own life just because it is at the
same time you own life. Life which could not be without you
. . . Accept what the other gives to you not only of himself but
of yourself. Love is as much a receiving, an accepting, as it is a
giving. The depth of your giving will be determined by your
receiving. There are things in you that you have never dreamed
of and they will be discovered to you by the one who now lives
his life for you. Accept it, accept the other, accept yourself . . .

. . . The world is indifferent to love, scornful of love, making play with love, unbelieving in love, because it cannot believe in God. The seeds of this indifference and unbelief lie
rooted also in *your* hearts.

Love is full of faith but we must ever make its faithfulness
our own, so that our varied and subtle fickleness achieves no
importance of itself. You will each of your need the faithfulness
of the other to sustain you against your own fickleness, your
own indifference and habit, your own feelings of guilt.

Love is suffering.

Love pushes life to its limits. The joys of being with and
for another bring you into areas of suffering born in the silent
places of the togetherness, unspoken and unspeakable. Areas

20. For the sake of the later generations who probably would not grasp this
nuance, the reader should be assured that every person among the hundred or
so present would immediately have understood that the pronoun 'he' and its
derivatives included both sexes—i.e., it means "the human being," male and
female; concretely in this situation it meant "both of you, Doug and Rhoda"!

where suffering and joy seem to interchange and intertwine as do pain and pleasure. Don't shun the suffering or try to banish it or escape from it. It is of love itself and will bring you to even fuller and freer relationship. There are no limits to your capacity for joy or suffering or relatedness. The limits you establish will—in love—be constantly broken down and transformed into new levels of being. This will happen of itself and because you are vigilant for its happening.

You will each of you remain you, even in this relationship. In this love you will assert yourself against each other. Love is patient, but you are impatient—stubborn, selfish, deceitful. You will know resentment against each other and be full of self-pity in new and frightening ways. You will envy each other as you never envied anyone before and you will be unkind and hurtful.

For you are now involved in that which is bigger than yourself, which you cannot manage, direct and control without destroying. You must be purged again and again in order to learn to live not against but for and with each other.

Love does not stifle or possess but opens life.

There is no limit to love's faith, hope and endurance.

- your faith is full of shallows;

- your hope is ever failing

- your endurance all too quickly peters out.

But there is nothing love cannot face.

There is no limit to love's faith, hope and endurance.

This is not just some far-off beacon toward which, with more or less success, you have begun to struggle. This is the promise under which you have chosen to stand. Like a great, deeply-rooted tree it casts its protective shadow over the life you are proposing to live together.

Knowing your own limits, failings, fickleness, perversity, you are willing to trust more in its limitlessness. It will shelter you through your own faithlessness, recall you from your hopelessness, indifference and guilt, and give you an endurance not your own. There is nothing love cannot face and even your faithlessness, your hopelessness, your frailty cannot turn it away.

As your love takes root, it will become a refreshment and sheltering place not only for yourselves and your family but for the stranger who is so often without love . . .

This journey of love is the most important of your human existence. For this you were made and through this you are rooted and grounded to grow out from yourselves and to glimpse and participate in the root and ground of all human existence—love with and for the other . . .

In love we know most surely of our life and of Him who has given it. And we discover love most surely, most fully and most joyfully as we persevere in the suffering it brings us.

Do not flee or hide from one another and you will discover more of life and love than you have yet dreamed of.

He who does not love does not know God: for God is love.[21]

I have reproduced this much (not all) of Bob Miller's wedding sermon in order to give the reader some inkling of the depths of theological and human insight this "young Abelard," now forty years of age, had attained. Those who are familiar with the theological literature of the twentieth century will easily recognize in these thoughts the Kierkegaardian dialectic—the yes and no of love ("Love is exciting and troubling, joyful but awesome"); and the theocentrism of Barth ("To say God is love does not mean love is God"); and the Christian realism of Niebuhr ("the misery and triumph of human being"); and even, I think, the ontological sensibility of Tillich ("in love you will be transformed into new levels of being," etc.). Bob Miller had learned well what the best contemporary minds in the Christian movement had to teach us. But his was not a rote learning: he had appropriated these emphases and made them his own. It had passed, all of it, through the rough sieve of his own "living, dying and being damned."[22] I have often thought, as I read these words in later years, that their author understood what

21. Copied from the actual text of the sermon Robert Miller preached in Riverside Church on May 28, 1960.

22. Luther's definition of the work of theology.

marriage in a Christian context means far better than most who are married; and perhaps he understood it so profoundly because he was himself denied its comforts and its demands. Even today, as I copied and re-thought these sentences, I was grasped anew by their poignancy and their timeless wisdom. Bob Miller, as I have noted previously, is often remembered by others as a silent man— "the quiet Kierkegaardian," or even the "detached" and "apparently indifferent" one, as a well-known theologian said of him. But the limits and, in some cases, the falseness of that kind of *imago* are revealed quite patently by this testimony to the inner life of the man.

10

Rhoda and I spent the first three months of our life together in Halifax—she had agreed to work at the Dalhousie Library for the summer, and it was an opportunity for me to get to know her homeland, her family, and her old friends like George and Sheila Grant. In July a letter from Bob announced that his mother and Imogene Walker, a former SCMer and friend from Alberta, were making a trip to the Maritimes, and that he had given them our address. We both always enjoyed Mrs Miller, and were glad to see her and Imogene. The same letter contained a reference to the growing pace of work at the SCM Book Room, as did most of Bob's communications throughout these years. A little later on that summer he wrote, "We are really swamped these days with another big jump in business and five of us can't keep up with it all. And now in the middle of it I have a lovely head cold. We all seem to be getting them around here—our unhealthy big city life. I have been rolling around in bed all day and now sit here looking at stupid Ed Sullivan and his stupid show."

Knowing that we would be leaving soon for our first (and, as it turned out, only) parish—St Andrew's United Church in Blind River at the top of Lake Huron—he added: "Don't be too hard on the people. They are just people, but that's saying something." When I asked him in my reply what text he would suggest for my first sermon to my new congregation, he replied immediately (and decisively!): First Corinthians 1:18ff.: *For the word of the cross is folly to those who are perishing, but to us who are being saved it is the power of God . . . The foolishness of God is wiser than men, and the weakness of God is stronger than men . . . I decided to know nothing among you except Jesus Christ and him crucified. And I was with you in weakness and in much fear and trembling . . .* No better text could be found for a young and inexperienced preacher who had spent the past eleven years trying to become wise and eloquent of words! It was, besides, the *locus classicus* of the whole tradition to which my studies had led me, and which became, in fact, the core of my whole work as a teacher and writer of theology—what Luther named the "theology of the cross" (*theologia crucis*).

At first it was a little daunting for me, after living on Broadway for the past seven years, to learn again how to be the village boy who knew that you should smile at people when you met them on the street! But when, after two years in that remarkable lumbering town, where our first two children were born, we were loath to leave St Andrew's Church. But since by that time we had acquired, besides the children, a lovely little plot of Crown Land on one of the islands in "the Big Lake" (as everyone called Lake Huron), we have been able to return to that beautiful part of "the Near North" for fifty years by now; and many of the people who were our first and only parish have become old friends—"just people, but that's saying something!"

The church had asked me to become the first principal of a new, experimental college on the campus of the new, experimental university—the University of Waterloo. During the three years of our work at St. Paul's United College, there were visits from many old friends, including some who were also good friends of Bob Miller—like Rose and Emil Fackenheim, and George and Sheila Grant. But Bob himself, whose work ethic was classically 'Protestant,' could never become free enough to visit us, though on at least one occasion plans had been concretely laid. And then—

> This letter, I am sorry to say, will be a disappointment, for I am not coming to visit you. Things have not worked out for a continuous extended holiday and I just didn't feel up to a trip.

I have to get some real rest for my holiday or I am not much good. I drove Mother to Montreal to visit relatives for the better part of one week, and the drive down and back wore me out . . . Then I agreed to do a set of book reviews for *Christian Frontiers* on CBC.

I took some days off and looked into books. Then there was one week left and with that I am having a musical holiday. Paul Warner has a little third floor apartment without a telephone, but with a back sun porch and record player. So I have retired into it. Only there is no sun!

We have almost doubled our space at the office. We had a door put through the wall to the house on Sultan Street behind us. The Book Room has three rooms on the second floor, and the National office [of the SCM] on the third floor.

In the Book Room next year, in addition to Charlotte, Beverley Peterson and myself, there will be Paul Warner, John Anderson, David Girling and half time Larry Goudge and Gladys Rivere (Don Wilson's sister-in-law). We shall also be running the Book store for the new university, York, and there will be another fellow in charge of that. I shouldn't even be writing about it all, because it makes me meditate on how much there is going to be to do before term opens.

That letter ends on a new note: "I am starting to read about music, too—a hobby for my declining years!" I remembered that Bob had told me once that, during his travels as SCM Study Secretary, he had agreed to be part of the famous experiments with L.S.D. of Doctors Abram Hoffer and Humphrey Osmond at the mental hospital in Weyburn, Saskatchewan and in Saskatoon. Bob said that during his hours under the influence of this so-called "psychedelic drug" he had listened to classical music—and had ever since then known a much more intensive relationship with music.[23] In fact, Bob's relation to music, I have sometimes thought, could become at least a *leitmotiv* of any attempt to write his biography. Even before his retirement he was fond of, and knowledgeable about, opera in particular. He shared this love of opera with

23. Richard Allen told me that he believes Bob wrote something about this experience; but we have not been able to locate it.

his cousin, Mary McInroy, who writes, "It was when I was nursing in Toronto that Bob and I found that we had a common interest in music, especially opera! We would travel to a predetermined café for a supper visit, each of us by streetcar, and then take in concerts at Massey Hall, the O'Keefe Centre, and elsewhere. I travelled with the Canadian Opera Company to Europe and the USA, and two years ago to St Petersburg. It was Bob who encouraged me to do this. He would say, "Oh, just *go!* Don't miss it!"[24]

He also kept reminding me that music was my own 'native homeland,' too. Once, when I was giving some lectures in the Toronto School of Theology, he told one of the students who dropped into the Bob Miller Book Room to tell Douglas Hall not to forget the piano and composition! In 1995, responding to something I had written him about the importance of music in our family life, Bob wrote: "glad to have that report about piano playing. It's where you began, and where you need to end. All this other stuff is child's play. Real play is other, as I'm sure R. knows, as do your kids!" The evolution of the importance of music in Bob's life could be an illustration of the well-known aphorism of Water Pater that "All art constantly aspires to the condition of music."

In 1965 there was an opening to teach in my own field of systematic theology at one of the most interesting theological colleges of our denomination, St Andrew's College in the University of Saskatchewan at Saskatoon. Since such opportunities were extremely rare in Canada, I felt that I had to accept it, despite my reluctance to leave St Paul's United College after just three years. I suppose I could have excused myself by noting that the average duration of university and college headship in North America at that time was just about three years (a statistic that speaks volumes about the tumultuous nature of the times!) But I had greatly enjoyed helping to get St Paul's started, and could only justify my departure on the grounds of wishing to begin in a serious way practicing the discipline for which I had been trained. The board was very gracious and sent us off to the West with many expressions of goodwill.

24. Letter of April 2010.

We had only been in Saskatoon for three months when a letter from Bob Miller announced the death of one of his (and Rhoda's) good friends: the Reverend Bev. Burwell, an Anglican priest, who had been SCM campus secretary at the University of Manitoba and was at the time of his death managing a branch of the SCM Book Room in Hamilton: "He had of course been working much too hard at the book room—just as he always did," Bob wrote. "It has been thriving in its new location and he enjoyed it very much and was pleased with the success he was making of it." We knew that Bev's death was a personal blow to Bob, for he had high regard for the integrity and wisdom of this good man.

The same letter contained news of George and Sheila Grant and their children; they had taken up residence in a huge old mansion on the edge of Dundas, Ontario, when George began his work as head of the religion department at MacMaster University. "I called on the Grants while I was in Dundas, and they were asking after you, and very pleased to hear about Sara Irene [our third child, who was born in Saskatoon just after our arrival there]. They both remarked on how delightful it had been to visit you in your own home [in Waterloo] and to see the pleasure you had in your children and your life together."[25]

A little earlier, I had written to Bob about certain changes that I felt were beginning to occur in my thinking as a result of my encounter with the specifics of the prairie context in which I now found myself. It was a change that continued apace for several years, and it resulted, in the end, in a new sense of the importance of *context* for Christian theology. I realized gradually that I could not pursue that kind of epistemology without raising questions about Karl Barth's kerygmatic approach to faith, and, somewhat to my surprise, I began to develop a new appreciation for the teacher with whom I had struggled most at Union Seminary: Paul Tillich.[26] I suspected that Bob might look askance at such a development, and I was not wrong: "I can see," he wrote in November of 1965,

25. Letter of December 6, 1965.

26. I have written about this in an article for the series "How My Mind Has Changed" in the *Christian Century*.

"that you are already retreating into a theological haze of prairie sameness. The Tillichian valleys and the Barthian mountain tops are being levelled and made plain, as the refrain goes. I can see that you are going to cross Mr [Kenneth] Hamilton."[27]

The same letter again remarks on the joys and sorrows of the Book Room, which was the core concern of Bob Miller's whole life. "Work here continues as busy as ever, or more so, and I try desperately to hold my collapsing staff together in a reasonable semblance of wholeness. Many of them live with great problems, which erupt all over the place—especially when we get very busy. It is something like an out-patient clinic without a therapeutist [*sic*]."

The letter ends with the news that "Nettie and Dick Allen are expecting in the new year. If you are ever in Regina be sure to look them up. They would be very happy to see you."

Shortly after that, another, longer letter was headed "Mid-Atlantic, 33,000 ft. up":

Dear Rhoda and Doug:

It being spring, you'll know that the wanderlust has afflicted me, and here I am 'high' (it's only a rum and coke!). My journeys also always have to have some 'high' (like marriage) purpose. This time it is different. I have been invited to sit on the Christian Literature Fund Committee of the World Council of Churches, which is meeting for five days in May in Lausanne. This is an independent committee which is given 2–3 million dollars by the World Council with no strings attached, and the Committee is to spend it in the developing countries on projects which it sees fit to subsidize. The project must have to do with indigenous literature—writing, printing, distributing, selling, etc., or any phase of such. The Committee is to exist for five years and to spend all its money by that time. This is the second meeting. I have no idea how they lighted on me to fill the place of Max Warren, who is ill. I have even less idea what I have to contribute. I cannot see any relevance of anything that we do. Nor am I a well-functioning committee man. However, I said

27. Hamilton was professor of theology at the University of Winnipeg, and an avid Barthian as well as interpreter of the novels of John Updike.

I'd try, so here I am. And of course it is to be a holiday, with a few days in London (Covent Garden, I hope) and other exciting events including a lengthier visit with the Flessemans and a shorter one with Mrs Douglas in Ireland on the way home.

I trust that this explanation will be accepted for the brief pause that there will be in the sending of sprouting literature on the Death of God and other revolting contemporary theology. I left some instructions on your behalf. Glad to hear you are so much enjoying Saskatoon.

The letter had been set aside then until the flight had touched down in Amsterdam and Bob was once again in the home of his good Dutch friends:

Am now at Flesseman's, after pushing my way about in the travelling hordes. As someone said, travelling has replaced revolution as the activity of the masses. Tourism is the most important factor in today's world. If Viet Nam north and south would open their doors to the tourists, the war would soon be over!

I am now reading my documents and trying to decide whether we need a printing press in Bangalore, a wireless conference in Sarawak, a mobile book van in Kitwe, and how to be a Christian agriculturalist in the Swahili dialect or . . . or . . . Our little project on St Thomas Street doesn't somehow throw any light [on these subjects], and I am wondering whether I am going to be more than a tourist on this trip.

Ellen is well and working hard at all sorts of projects here in the local church and in the WCC Faith and Order Commissions. Some day I can tell you what there is to tell about Calvin's Sermons on Ephesians. It is at any rate classed genuinely as a rare book.[28]

28. This refers to a wonderful gift that Bob had sent us—Calvin's Ephesians sermons, in English, published in 1577, just thirteen years after Calvin's death. Its margins are filled with minute and beautifully scripted notes, presumably by some Presbyterian minister or scholar, in some past century. Bob had acquired the book quite by accident when he was rummaging through old books in a used bookstore in Edinburgh during his year of study there. He discovered later that it is one of only four copies still in existence.

11

Our correspondence with Bob Miller was sporadic over the next few years. He was increasingly taken up with the "booming" Book Room project, the Howland Avenue co-operative-living community,[29] and his concern for his brother and his mother. And we were increasingly immersed in the academic life of St Andrew's College and its related institutions, and of course with our own growing family. I had begun to be involved in various national committees of the United Church, however, and, a little later, with guest lectures here and there; and whenever my or our travels took us to Toronto or its environs, as happened every summer, too, with our long trek from Saskatoon to our island property in Algoma, we usually had brief visits with Bob, whether alone or with mutual friends.

There was, among these, a quite lively (intensive would be better, probably) visit with him and Paul at the home of our good friends Rose and Emil Fackenheim during the Easter season of 1971. Evelyn Reid was present—and in mourning. A letter we'd received from Bob a little earlier had been written on the day of Doug Reid's death in New York City: October 23, 1970.

> We are like those families who only come together for calamities.
>
> Doug Reid died this morning.

29. I have intentionally avoided discussing the Howland Avenue cooperative, partly because my knowledge of that community is limited (though I visited there on two or three occasions and knew some of the people involved), and partly because it remains a rather controversial topic. It began with good intentions all around, but, as with so many experiments in communal living, it was not sufficiently realistic, I think, about individual needs and conflict management. Financially the experiment was facilitated by Gladys Miller's willingness to sell her own home in exchange for the kind of friendship and care she hoped to find among her son's friends and associates. I am sure that many good things came of the experiment, but in the end it proved at best ambiguous and at worst a painful episode in Bob Miller's own life. I know that the Howland Avenue experience is being written up by Elizabeth Anderson, whose parents, John and Muriel, were part of the community.

You likely know that he had some form of leukemia, and Evelyn has been aware for about three years that it couldn't be cured. Doug never admitted to her, the doctor, or anyone that he knew what was really the matter with him.

They spent a very pleasant weekend at the Mill [a country place Bob and Paul Warner had renovated]. They went for a holiday on the east coast and had a long weekend with the Powickes'—at least Evelyn did. I think Doug was in the hospital at the time.

I phoned Evelyn this morning. Doug had picked up this fall and then in the last week had . . . agreed reluctantly to go back to Hospital. They sat up all night talking because he couldn't sleep and they were waiting for the ambulance, and he went about 8 a.m. She's keeping him at home, and he will be buried from the church on Tuesday, 6 p.m. I think I shall go down.[30]

As I've already noted, Bob did go down to New York, and stayed with Evelyn and their children for a whole week. The evening at the Fackenheims' was therefore a poignant one for us all: Rhoda and Rose had both been tenants of the Reids in the 1950s when Doug had been Ray McCleary's associate at WoodGreen, and Rhoda felt particularly close to Evelyn.

The evening was also memorable because of a vigorous discussion between the Fackenheims and Rhoda and me, which became surprisingly spirited and rather too personal. The Fackenheims—Rose in particular—argued passionately that the Holocaust was absolutely unique in the whole history of racial hatred and 'ethnic cleansing.' No human suffering could be compared with the (Christendom-inspired) Nazi attempt to eradicate the Jews. This had become one of their primary themes (some, like our mutual friend Gregory Baum, would say 'obsessions'), and Rhoda and I, despite our long-standing friendship with Rose and Emil, felt that their position was excessive. My own theological teaching and writing had been profoundly affected by the literature of the

---

30. Letter from 105 Howland Avenue, Toronto, October 23, 1970.

Holocaust, especially that of Elie Wiesel;[31] and I was astonished now to hear Emil claim Wiesel as his primary ally in this approach. He and Rose made any denial of their position a tacit concession to Nazism—giving Hitler a "posthumous victory." Rhoda and I were astounded at the intensity with which both Fackenheims advanced this argument, for, bound up as it was in their unconditional support of the State of Israel, it seemed to us not only to exclude from human consideration every other suffering people, but also, in the present historical context, to preclude any criticism of modern Israel. At its height, the "discussion" seemed to me almost an attack on us personally, or as representatives of the Christian religion. It puzzled us even more that Bob Miller remained completely neutral in the discussion, or seemed so. I had known for years that he had a strong feeling for the role of the Jewish people in history, and especially for its *parental* relationship vis-à-vis the "grafted-on branch" of Christianity [see Romans 11]. But so had (and have!) I. I persuaded myself, however, that Bob's silence on the occasion was due to the complexity of his relationship with Rose and Emil, his immense respect for them both, and his wish to avoid the kind of alienation among friends that might have ended the evening.[32]

31. Rose had acknowledged this quite explicitly in an earlier letter to us: "thank you, Doug, for your good letter, which I only now received . . . In fact it was such a nice letter that I would have been tempted to share parts of it with Elie [Wiesel] when he was here last Sunday, had I had it then—the parts about what you are doing in your classes. Your choices are excellent. I am curious as to how your students are affected by such readings as *A Plea for the Dead*. A few years ago, a chap at Trinity decided to do his undergrad course on religion on the subject of prejudice. He began by making his students read [Wiesel's novel] *Night*. According to one of them, a mature S.C.M. secretary, it fell completely flat and the kids couldn't wait to get on with the real issue—blacks" [Letter of February 5, 1970]

32. I ought to have remembered something what Rose Fackenheim had written in her long letter of February 5, 1970: "As for the Holocaust, we haven't begun to face up to it. We don't dare. It is too frightening. As a certain Rev. [Bob] Miller said in an excellent sermon, after what we [Christians] have done, it is almost indecent for us now to listen in on the Jew's anguished questioning of and quarrel with God. Rather, we must review all of our history and all of our theology from the perspective of the holocaust, and perhaps all we will be left with is the God is Dead theology!"

As it was, we all parted amicably, though with many unresolved thoughts.

Some time later, Bob included in a shipment of books to us in Saskatoon a note in which he remarked, "Your friend [and former colleague, Robert] Bater was just here. Rose is impressed. She went to his Easter service and he quoted concentration-camp poetry. He is having Gregory Baum to talk about Jewish-Christian relations [at his Toronto church]." I knew, however, that Gregory would have opinions that Rose would not find as compatible as she thought Bob Bater's were.

There was, however, an important sequel to our historic evening with our friends. While Rhoda and I could not follow the Fackenheims in their Jewish exceptionalism, we never doubted the depths and importance of Emil's work both as a philosopher and a theologian. When in 1972, just prior to our first major sabbatical leave in Germany, the committee on honourary degrees at St Andrew's College considered the perennial matter of whom to offer such a degree at its forthcoming spring convocation, I was instrumental in persuading the committee that it would be very appropriate for us to give the degree, Doctor of Divinity *honoris causa,* to the greatest contemporary Jewish thinker in Canada, Emil Fackenheim. For many of us in Christian academic circles, I argued, Fackenheim has been helping us to regain an informed sense of the importance of our Jewish roots and of our vital and ongoing connectedness with Judaism. There was sufficient support for this proposal that it was passed by the board of the college. However, in the volatile circumstances of the nearly incendiary and media-enflamed disputation between the editor of the *United Church Observer,* Al Forrest, and Fackenheim and his supporters, this led to an immediate crisis for the College and its supporters. The media, depending on their specific policies and prejudices, assumed that the action of St Andrew's constituted a vindication of Fackehneim or (as Forrest himself put it) a "slap in the face" to the denomination's primary publication, and we found ourselves simultaneously hated and feted by persons and organizations all across the country. Then, after the decision to offer Emil an honourary D.D. had already been made, the College's board itself was so swayed by one of its members, a personal friend of the Editor of the *Observer*, that it convened a special meeting to discuss whether the invitation should be revoked—on the very day that the Fackenheims were *en route* to Saskatoon for the convocation! Fortunately for me, the students of the College were entirely behind the original decision of the Committee, and there was sufficient support (and no doubt embarrassment!) on the board that that decision was upheld.

Perhaps I, and others who had initiated this action, had been a little naïve in not foreseeing the crisis that might well be evoked by such a move. Unfortunately, in both Christian and Jewish popular circles, Emil Fackenheim was known chiefly, if not exclusively, for his support of Israel in the face of the sufferings of Palestine.[33] I have included in this account the discussion our evening with the Fackenheims and Miller and others in order to show that we, too, had questions about the exclusivity of the Fackenheim position. But we intended the honour as an act of peacemaking, which for some it really was, not a cause for further strife; and we intended it as a 'statement' about Emil Fackenheim's *scholarship* and its singular importance to Canadian Christian theological understanding.

I confess, however, that I am still somewhat perplexed by Bob Miller's complete silence during that discussion, for he must have known that Rhoda and I would agree wholeheartedly with his sensitive awareness of Christian culpability in relation to the Holocaust.

In the same letter that contains his reference to Bob Bater, Bob Miller writes, "I suppose your papers featured the Toronto columnist who called Saskatoon the Kitsch centre of Canada." Since we knew several of the excellent artists in our city, we were properly incensed by this all-too-typical Eastern snobbery and knew that Bob was teasing us for our new admiration for 'the West.' Perhaps this reference to art prompted him to report that "My friend Olga

33. Actually, Emil was by no means wholly uncritical of Israel, but he felt that such criticism needed to be made from a position *inside* the state of Israel itself; and indeed it was partly for that reason that he and Rose and their children emigrated to Israel after his retirement from the University of Toronto.

Douglas,[34] who died last Fall, left behind 169,666 unsorted paintings, sketches, etc., etc. I have taken on the job of deciding what
can be sold and what we should keep, and trying to find inexpen-
sive ways of presentation. I'm becoming expert on pictures, mat-
ting, etc.!" It's almost mind-boggling to contemplate l69,666 pieces
of art, and we admired our friend's willingness to sort them out.

In 1972 in a letter just dated "Wednesday"[35] Bob wrote to
Rhoda to tell her of the death of Ted (the Reverend Edward) Nichols, SCM general secretary during the period when Rhoda was
national missions secretary. Ted Nichols had been a conscientious
and imaginative head officer of the Movement in Canada, and had
managed to set it on a good financial footing; he was also a very
good friend of both Bob and Rhoda, as well as many others. Bob
wrote: "The enclosed is sad news. It was, I gather, a heart attack.
Hilda Powicke has gone to the funeral and memorial service [in
Vancouver], both to be with Ruby [Ted's wife] and to represent
old S.C.M. connections. We are raising a little money now to finance that, and are talking about some other project to which
people might contribute—maybe in connection with the S.C.M.
Any ideas?"

The same letter included one from Rose Fackenheim. It contained a lovely, humourous reference to the recent St Andrew's
College convocation at which Emil had received his (controversial!) DD Emil's address on the occasion was a stirring one. When
it ended, the students of the College rose in a body and applaud-
ed—which felt like a vindication to those of us who had gone out
on that particular limb! But what had impressed our 12-year-old
daughter Katie most was not the address, but the way that Rosie
made her way down the aisle of Knox Church that evening,
dressed in a "swishy long dress and clicky heels," the essence, in
Katie's eyes, of big-city sophistication. Rose said she hoped she

---

34. The Canadian artist and wife of George Vibert Douglas, who started
the Department of Geology at Dalhousie University, and who had returned to
her family home in Sligo, Ireland, after her husband's death.

35. Bob's later letters were frequently vague as to their dates, though I can
usually detect the specifics from their content.

could make that sort of entrance again one day in Katie's presence! She also told Rhoda that she "Definitely recommended" travelling with "speechifying husbands." Bob commented to Rhoda: "You must begin to follow Rose's example (though I don't approve when she does it [since she had to leave her work at the Book Room], I would when you did it." Unfortunately this didn't become possible until our children had become a little older, and by then our home base had changed.

12

In 1974 I was offered the chair of Christian theology at McGill University's Faculty of Religious Studies. We had been in Saskatoon for almost a decade, and it had become home for all of us, especially our four children, who enjoyed their life in the Saskatoon French School and their many other activities. I was reluctant to leave St Andrew's College, too. It has been one of the more theologically-alert and politically active institutions of our denomination, and in the past four or five years I had become increasingly involved with other faculties of the large University of Saskatchewan. But Montreal and McGill had many things to offer us at this stage in our family life, not least of all the so-called French Fact. We decided to go. Bob wrote: "Sure you'll be glad you moved. You'll all hate it for ever so long. You'll pine for dear old Saskatoon. But you'll all get over it, and you'll all be grateful for all the good advice you got from your friends."

Not long after we had received that letter—it was the spring of 1975—the deplorable and (I would not say "tragic," as some do, but) pathetic debacle known as the SCM Book Store disaster broke out. For Rhoda and me, it was quite literally a shock. We were reading before sleep one night in our house on Temperance Street in Saskatoon and there was a late phone call. It was a young friend of ours, whom we had known since her childhood. We liked her very much, as we did her parents and siblings; we were all close friends. That is what made the phone call so bizarre and, finally, so shocking. After a little chitchat, the young woman began speaking in an alarmed, somewhat strident and eventually very emotional manner about a "terrible man" who was destroying the very fabric of the SCM. She was to become the national SCM's student president that year and had just returned from a Toronto meeting of the student executive. She reported that this unfeeling, grasping, capitalistic person, the Book Steward, was refusing to allow the student organization any "say" in the operation of the Book Room. She was filled with righteous indignation. It seemed quite inconsistent with her usually temperate and pleasant character.

In the midst of her outburst, Rhoda and I suddenly realized that the young woman was talking about our old friend, Bob Miller! Then, I am afraid, we both exploded. "Wait a minute, my dear," I said, "You are talking about a man whom we have known for many years. He is a very close friend of ours. What you are saying about him makes absolutely no sense to us!" And so on. The conversation quickly devolved, then, into a most unhappy conflict, with our young friend weeping and we ourselves nearly speechless. We were really "in shock."

I am going to leave any more reflective consideration of this entire episode for later (chapter 4). For the present, I will simply report that it marks, for us and for many others, a lasting and very sad alteration in our relationship with the SCM—effectively, I would say, it marks the end of the SCM as we had known it, and as it had been for hundreds of Canadian university students and senior advisors for about sixty years. What emerged from the crisis was a shadow of what had been—for a few, I gather, a courageous little band, but for those of us who had known the SCM in the 1940s and 1950s a pathetically attenuated and marginalized organization, conspicuously lacking in the breadth of concern, depth of commitment to the university, and a practically nonexistent relationship with the churches.

The cause and the course of this devastating break-up of a movement that had been so significant in our lives and the lives of many are too complex to discuss in this present narrative approach to the life of Robert W. Miller. To explain them would require, I have always felt, a very gifted and sensitive novelist—someone of the calibre of Dostoevsky or Thomas Mann! For now, I shall summarize the stages of the conflict in four brief observations:

First, the SCM Book Room evolved, not as a corporate project of the Canadian SCM, but as the vision of one person. It was, namely, the concretization of Bob Miller's growing sense, as study secretary, that Canadian universities and Canadian churches were woefully lacking in a well-planned and accessible source of contemporary theological and other relevant literature. When, after six years, Bob left the study secretariat of the movement, he set himself the task of creating such an outlet. As the reader will have detected in one or two of the excerpts I have quoted early from Bob's letters, it soon became evident that the kind of financial resources needed for an adequate book store would prove a drain on the SCM finances; so, in a verbal agreement between Miller, the national secretary of the time (Ted Nichols), and the board, it was determined that the Book Store, while remaining under the nomenclature of the Movement,[36] would operate as an *independent* entity. The truth is, I think, that at this point Bob was the only one who believed a success could be made of such a venture; the others involved, while appreciative of the idea, were quite sceptical of its viability. In fact, the other partners in this agreement told Bob straightforwardly, "You're on your own." They were happy as individuals to lend their moral support to Bob's idea, but as conscientious representatives of the SCM of Canada they did not want to run the risk of a costly business failure.

Second, the Book Room didn't fail, but (as references to the venture in Bob's to letters to Rhoda and me confirm) it gradually overcame the challenges that it quite naturally encountered, and finally it exceeded everyone's expectations, including Bob's. Bob found among his acquaintances and others a number of persons who were willing to invest money in the venture.[37] The Book Store

36. Similarly, the SCM Press of Britain, while maintaining the nomenclature of the Movement, was a completely independent organization.

37 . Mary McInroy was one of them. She writes: "I made my donation of $2000, interest free, and it was re-paid before a year had passed" (letter to me, March-April 2010).

could count on a loyal clientele throughout Canada and beyond; it acquired a large stock of books, necessitating various moves to more expansive quarters as well as an increased staff; and, as many testified, it achieved an excellent reputation for knowledgeable and helpful service among university teachers, students and clergy, as well as the general public. Its success, as nearly everyone realized, was due chiefly to Bob Miller. He knew books; he cared about the customers; he worked with unheard-of dedication and for minimal remuneration; and he trained a cadre of persons who, though never without tensions and personal struggles,[38] were in the main "a team." While the national SCM was kept informed about the operations of the Book Store, the independence of the latter was honoured, and on the whole good will between the Store and the umbrella organization prevailed over the years.

Third, the breakdown of this mutuality began, unnoticed, with the spirit of dissatisfaction and unrest which occurred throughout the Western world in the 1960s and, as I shall show in part 4, exercised a particularly conspicuous influence in universities. The impact of this so-called countercultural revolution was not seriously felt in the Canadian SCM until the 1970s, though (as I shall argue presently) it could be noticed in subtle ways in the sixties. In the early and mid-1970s, influenced by a few of the more vociferous student leaders and the vigorous (some said "crusading") determination of the new General Secretary, Mr Alan Rimmer,[39]

38. See his comment on this on page X-REF.

39. Alan Rimmer, whom I knew a little, was an affable youngish Englishman who became the general secretary of the SCM of Canada. Although I do not know whether his interest in the SCM was rooted in his earlier experience, I always felt that his affiliation with the Canadian SCM was rather more coincidental than vital and intentional. His personal charm cannot be denied, and it easily endeared him to students and to some of the older friends of the Movement.

Clearly enough, he very soon identified Bob Miller as "the problem," and since Rimmer's particular aim was to resolve the financial crisis the Movement was facing, he felt, I think, that Bob's "paternalistic" hold on the (successful!) Book Room was preventing the SCM from claiming its "rightful" share of the Book Room's profits. While this could be interpreted in ideological terms, the economic background cannot be overlooked. It is clear from Mr Rimmer's to "rebuild" the Movement along more "socially engaged" lines, the full force of the demand for change was brought to bear on the Book Store. This rather sudden interest of the SCM leadership in the Book Room was no doubt inspired, in part, by the realization of the Movement's growing financial crisis; but it was articulated mainly in ideological terms, namely, as a need for a radical "democratization" of the Book Store. The agitating segment alleged that the Book Store had been operating as a 'capitalist' venture, conceived in outrageously "paternalistic" terms. This situation, so contrary to the spirit of the SCM, it was argued, should be replaced immediately by a truly "democratic," "socially useful" pattern of government and mission, in which the student-run Movement was represented at every level of the Book Store's operation.

Inevitably, these demands were rejected by the Book Steward and a large portion of his staff, since they were seen (rightly!) both to ignore the legally independent status of the Book Room, and to manifest an appalling naivety about the actual operation of such an enterprise. An enterprise as complex and nuanced as the provision of specialized literary resources for the academic and ecclesiastical communities of Canada could not be left in the hands of inexperienced amateurs, especially a student community whose fluidity and impermanence preclude wise, long range and consistent oversight. The Book Store had succeeded precisely because of the wisdom, personal devotion and plain hard work of the man who was now being derided as 'paternalistic', 'a capitalist', a person incapable of cooperation and dialogue, etc., etc.

---

memoranda at the time that he saw his primary task as that of extricating the Movement from a looming financial crisis.

Had the general secretary of the SCM at this critical moment in its history been more knowledgeably aware of the history of the Book Room *and* more sympathetic towards the Book Room's longstanding mission to its Canadian constituency, the entire debacle might have been averted. And precisely that was the message (harangue?) with which Rhoda and I greeted Alan Rimmer when he stopped off in Saskatoon on his way to the National Council of the SCM in Edmonton in May 1975—the Council that put the final touches to the alienation that had developed between the SCM and the Book Room under Bob Miller's stewardship.

What was occurring here—and of course not only here, but throughout society—was the ascendency of a simplistic and truncated conception of democracy. Democracy in its best and most workable expressions never meant that the *demos* ought to determine every actual or possible decision and action. Such a thing—sometimes called "direct democracy"—in fact constitutes a corruption and debasement of the democratic principle, for it leads to government, not by representation, but by referendum— and almost inevitably to social chaos. Nor does democracy, as practiced in the older democracies, imply the rejection of individual initiative. Today, after some very tragic world events, it is understood even in once-ironclad-communistic lands (even China) that individual genius, giftedness and energy are necessary to the welfare of many if not all facets and functions of a society. A truly democratic society is one that tries to combine individual talent and initiative with justice and active vigilance for the well-being of the whole.

Fourth, reading again the large accumulation of memos, reports, and sundry accounts of this unfortunate crisis, one realizes rather soon that the two approaches were basically incompatible and irreconcilable. Reconciliation was made even more improbable by the bitterness that accompanied the debate, and, in some cases, the duplicity and personal resentment of individuals. For years the SCM of Canada had withstood pressure groups within and without that wanted to turn it into a strictly confessional Christian or, alternatively, an equally confessional secular organization. Despite these, it had remained a *Movement,* that is, a flexible and welcoming forum where many positions and preferences could co-exist—and in that respect a community quite unique in Canadian universities. Now, it appeared, the demand for a political orthodoxy reputedly of 'the Left' had put an end to this admirable historic openness and inclusivity.

Throughout the country, people lined up on one side of the 'issue' or the other;[40] long friendships were wounded or permanently damaged; and there emerged from the dust a strange, false

40

and (I fear) lasting image of Bob Miller that still leaves me gasping. It is an image that has nothing whatsoever in common with the Bob Miller I met long ago on Beausoleil Island, the man who conveyed to me a liberating message that altered the course of my life, and who continued to reinforce that message, in one way or another, until his death in 2003. I am writing this essay for him—and for myself. I should like to discredit for ever, if possible, that terrible image of the "terrible man."

For many senior friends of the SCM throughout Canada, however, Ramsay Cook, well-known history professor at the University of Toronto, summarized our assessment of the situation in a letter to the *Globe and Mail* in early March, 1975:

> It is impossible to express adequately the dismay and depression I experienced on reading the account of the resignation of Rev. Robert Miller as manager of the Student Christian Movement of Canada Book Room . . . What a disaster for Toronto readers, and especially for those thousands of students who have benefited so much from Bob Miller's extraordinary devotion to books and book distribution.
>
> Twenty years ago, Bob Miller's ill-equipped room in an old Bloor Street house (long since replaced by some concrete monster) was about the only place in Toronto where requests for specialized academic books were treated seriously. Since then the book-selling trade has much improved, but even now there is no match for the SCM Book Room when it comes to knowledge of books, efficient service and just plain courtesy. And the reason is simple: Bob Miller read and appreciated books himself, and he trained a staff in that fine, and disappearing, tradition.
>
> It would be impossible to estimate the contribution that Bob Miller's SCM Book Room has made to the intellectual and cultural life not only of Toronto, but to the country at large, for it has many mail-order customers. One thing is certain, and that is that there are thousands of students who will be disappointed . . .
>
> To that one must sadly add that Mr. Miller's Book Room was about the only thing that kept the Student Christian

Movement from becoming a completely bizarre circus in these last years. Appalling evidence of the quality of the recent leadership of that organization can be found in Allan Rimmer's self-righteous account of his conflict with Mr. Miller. A mind filled more with moralistic clichés and goofy fantasies would be difficult to imagine. That its owner should be allowed to undermine what amounts to Bob Miller's lifework fills me with despair, to say nothing of rage.

13

Perhaps the warning signs of the coming catastrophe were already visible, for those who had eyes to see, at the time of the Fiftieth Anniversary of the Canadian SCM in 1969, at Bolton, Ontario. A mood of vague dissatisfaction, generational mistrust and ideological fervour on the part of a minority were certainly present there; but then-General Secretary Roy DeMarsh and other genial and thoughtful people (like Marie-Jeanne and John Coleman, Mary (Rowell) Jackman, Verne Wishart, Rick and Liz Neufeld, Brian Fraser, and others) were able to make their presence felt in such a way as to defuse any incipient breakdown of civility. I felt it, though, as did my friend, the Protestant chaplain of the University of Muenster, Westphalia, Dr Friedrich Hufendiek, who had come along with us as a family. I had been asked to deliver the main lectures on the occasion. Later, without any prompting on my part, they were picked up by the World Student Christian Federation in Geneva, then under the leadership of the Finnish theologian Risto Lehtonen, which published them under the title *Hope against Hope*.[41] It was my first longer publication, and it became a kind of precursor for my first major book, *Lighten Our Darkness: Towards an Indigenous Theology of the Cross*.[42] As such, it was promoted actively by Willem Visser 't Hooft, the former General Secretary

41. Douglas John Hall, *Hope against Hope* (Geneva: WSCF, 1972).

42. *Lighten Our Darkness: Towards an Indigenous Theology of the Cross* (Philadelphia: Westminster, 1976; revised and enlarged edition by David Monge; Lima, OH: Academic Renewal, 2001).

of the World Council of Church, who was still very active in ecumenical and student work. I doubt, however, that the WSCF publication was ever studied (or even known?) in the Canadian SCM, apart from a few stalwarts—though I know it was stocked by the Book Room!

That does not surprise me, because I had already sensed a disconcerting whiff of rejection at the anniversary in Bolton. I interpreted that partly as an all too characteristically Canadian reaction to "one of our own"—the Who Do You Think You Are? syndrome identified by Alice Munro, who experienced it herself in her prefame days. But it was also a reaction to the *content* of my three lectures. They drew on George Grant's social analysis in *Philosophy in the Mass Age, Technology and Empire, Time as History,* and other works, and on various other social studies. Canadians are glad to critique the USA for its technocratic and triumphalistic ways, but we do not like to have such criticism levelled at our own "true north strong and free" (as witness Mr Michael Ignatieff's recent, politically inspired castigation of his more perceptive uncle, George Grant!).[43] My lectures were also inspired by the recent (and in Canada then scarcely known) theological groundbreaker, Jürgen Moltmann's *Theology of Hope.*[44] But I was already conscious then of the way that Moltmann's difficult book was being used, where it was known, in the North American context: few, I think, actually read it; the slogan was enough! In this 'New World' the chattering classes are full of optimism ("the religion of Progress," said George Grant, is our real religion), but *hope*, in the Christian sense, is something else again. It is hope *against* hope, against all the self-conscious, rhetorical and hyped-up cheeriness that is present in every television advertisement! In the biblical literature, hope is hope "on the other side of shipwreck" (Keats)—and only those who are courageous enough to enter the chaos and darkness of their lives and their epoch can see the light of *that* hope.

43. Michael Ignatieff, *True Patriot Love: Four Generations in Search of Canada* (Toronto: Viking Canada, 2009), ch. 4.

44. Jürgen Moltmann, *Theology of Hope*, trans. James W. Leitch (London: SCM, 1965).

Thus my carefully scripted lectures required not only close listening, but they introduced thoughts which, at both the theological and the socio-historical level, were difficult for many to swallow. The dominant religious or quasi-religious humour of the SCM was not, I think, as different from that of the liberal churches that had supported it as some SCMers liked to think. Religious liberalism, both in the form of an activistic "Social Gospel" and a pietistic spirituality, was still dominant—whether in old-fashioned 1930s form or in newer guises inspired by what a German friend of mine called "Woolworth Marxism." The great theological renewal mistakenly designated "neo-orthodoxy"—the work of Barth, Tillich, the Niebuhrs, Bonhoeffer, and the others; the teachers who had inspired Bob Miller and Ellen Flesseman and Jürgen Moltmann and many others somehow never reached most mainstream Protestant pews, and 'The Sixties' would witness its further displacement and disregard, so far as most churches in North America are concerned, through the rapid succession of 'theologies of' that commenced with the "revolting death of God theology" [Bob Miller], a plethora of liberation theologies developed among the poor of the earth (and therefore not demanding too much of us rich!), and then the various and noisy theologies of cause and identity, needful in their way, some of them, but finally distracting the churches from the need to think about their primary message (gospel) and its ethical imperatives *comprehensively* and in a fully *contextual mode* (something quite distinguishable from the contextual analyses within specific social groupings).

More, however, than any *specific* opposition to the ideas that I expressed at Bolton (in fact I remember *no* very specific complaints), what troubled me was that the whole mode of thought that we call *theology* seemed so foreign to this gathering of university people who, presumably, had been participants in an organization whose stated *raison d'etre* was the examination of the claims of the Christian faith and their meaning for the life of the world, notably the world of the university itself. Marie-Jeanne Coleman, Roy DeMarsh, Bob Bater, Verne Wishart, Fritz Hufendiek, and a few others who had (in some cases, but not all, professionally) been exposed to contemporary theology understood perfectly well what I was talking about; but the resistance that I sensed was not only a resistance to the ideas I expressed, and the language in which I expressed them, but to the whole exercise of trying to comprehend our world from the perspective of the Christian message, and of allowing that message to be tested and restated by the problems and possibilities of our here-and-now world. Most of those present, it seemed to me, were almost nonplussed by these lectures— lectures that were taken up by the international student body of which the Canadian SCM was a part, the WSCF. I felt many present were operating on some other wavelength—perhaps an *ethic-centred* passion in the more vocal persons, something religiously less well defined in others. *Theology* (by which I certainly do not mean "doctrine," but the kind of Christian imagination that wants, as Anselm said, to *understand what it believes*)[45] appeared to me as foreign a discipline to this apparently representative gathering of the Canadian SCM as it is to the churches at large, which have not had to "*do* theology" because the next generation would, they believed, quite naturally march obediently into the pews just vacated by the previous generation, age after age.

At the time, but more so in retrospect and in view of what transpired in the Canadian SCM in the mid-1970s, I wondered whether a movement that appeared so theologically empty and disinterested would not self-destruct as soon as its future was no longer assured by custom, economics, and the inspired leadership of a few. Whatever else Bob Miller may have been, he was a Christian whose faith had been evoked and sustained by *thinking*— theological thinking, which is also and simultaneously human personal and political thinking. As he said to me in many ways in several of his earliest letters particularly, "The church needs people who *think*"; and the absolute accuracy, indeed the *prophetic* accuracy of that emphasis, became more and more transparent as historical, biblical and theological thoughtlessness and amnesia

45. I have discussed the nature of theology in nearly all of my twenty-five or so books, so I shall not elaborate on this subject here. Those interested could turn to the first volume of my trilogy, *Thinking the Faith: Christian Theology in a North American Context* (Minneapolis: Fortress, 1989).

set into the ecclesiastical scene of mainstream Protestantism in the 1970s and beyond. The SCM at its best was never held together by adherence to doctrinal or creedal uniformity, *Deo gratia*; but it *was* held together by Christian theological discourse—*on the part of committed Christians but also on the part of those who did not or could not profess* that *Credo, but who wanted to find out what faith in Jesus as the Christ was all about, what it led to, what it abhorred, what it evoked by way of spirituality, morality and social passion.* That "centre did not hold" as the waves of secularism, consumerism and the various cultural wars broke over our society.[46] I wonder if the breakdown of the SCM whose visible catalyst *may* have been the book store fiasco had not already begun with the gradual and subtle, but not altogether invisible dissipation of purpose and centre that I felt at Bolton. Was the collapse of the Canadian SCM, at base, a failure of theology?

46. The reference is to the famous 1920 poem of W. B. Yeats. The poem explains much about the events that followed it in the twentieth century, including the turmoil of the Sixties, which was exemplified very concretely by the Book Store debacle: "Things fall apart, the centre cannot hold . . . The best lack all conviction, while the worst are full of passionate intensity . . . ," etc. The SCM at its best depended for its "centre" on a compassionate and worldly Christianity that could open itself to, and dialogue with, many world*views*, while maintaining a certain critical distance from all of them, including institutional Christianity. It was always difficult to walk the narrow path between "the little orthodoxies of the Left and the Right" (Orwell), and the Movement's natural orientation was, to be sure, to veer to the Left. But with the crisis that centred in the Book Store and its future the Movement actually *lurched* to the Left, or to a rhetorical and sloganized version thereof, so that those who felt compelled to stick to the Christian "centre" were effectively edged out.

Margaret Grant (Young)

Robert Miller

Ellen Flesseman-
van Leer

Paul Warner

Miller – McInroy Family Gathering
Back row: Henry Miller, Gladys Miller, unnamed friend
Front row: Alexander McInroy, Mary McInroy, Douglas Miller

National Council, S.C.M. of Canada, Guelph (Ontario)
Wm. Fennel and Margaret Prang – front row center
Marie-Jean deHaller [Coleman] – front right

Meg Young, 'Paddy,' Arthur Young, Bob Miller
Beausoleil Island, Georgian Bay, Summer 1948

'Beausoleil' 1948
Bob Miller back row 2nd from left; Douglas Hall front row left

Karl Barth (*top*)
Paul Tillich (*right*)

Reinhold Niebuhr (*top*)
John Coleman Bennett (*left*)

Hall – Palfrey Wedding Reception, May 28, 1960
Prophet's Chamber, Union Theological Seminary, NYC

Carol Vine and Robert Miller
The Bob Miller Book Room, Toronto

Emil Fackenheim and Rose [Komlodi] Fackenheim

Douglas John Hall and Rhoda [Palfrey] Hall

(*clockwise
from top*)
Ray McCleary,
George P. Grant,
Evelyn Reid

Gladys Miller and Imogene Walker
Halifax, Nova Scotia, Summer 1960

Rhoda Palfrey and Bob Miller
National Study Conference, Bala Ontario

**Leslie Peterson, Anglican
Bishop of Algoma (*top*)**

Richard Allen (*right*)

3

Beginning Again

1

ELIE WIESEL RELATES A rabbinic midrash that I greatly love: When God created human beings he gave them a special gift. It was not the possibility of *beginning*; only God can *begin*, creating *ex nihilo*. But their Creator gave the humans an even better gift: the ability to begin *again*![1]

Bob Miller had devoted himself to the Canadian SCM from 195l, when he assumed the role of study secretary for the Movement, until 1975, when he was forced out of the office of book steward (a concept and office he himself had created), which he had occupied since 1957. He had given the Movement twenty-four years of his life. The termination of his long, ill-paid, and devoted service to the Canadian SCM was infinitely more painful to him than to anyone else involved in the Book Store struggle. At the

---

1. Paul Warner reports that the very phrase was used when the group of loyal supporters surrounding Bob Miller decided to undertake a new venture—the one that became 'The Bob Miller Book Room': "It was Rose Fackenheim's suggestion that we leave the store and *begin again*. She felt that it was useless to try and work with the present SCM staff" (email to me on May 5, 2010).

height of the crisis, in a memorandum to the board of directors of
the SCM of Canada dated February 28, 1975, there is "cry of dere-
liction" that I cannot forget, nor can I remember anything like it in
all Bob's discourse: "Psychologically I can no longer function in relation to the present situation: quite simply, I don't eat properly, or
sleep properly, and certainly don't work properly, and hence I must
withdraw."[2] But while the conflict bruised and disillusioned him, it
did not make him bitter or cynical. Unlike most of us would have
done in his position, he did not indulge in a public display of re-
crimination, nor did he engage in malevolent accusations against
specific individuals. Indeed, as Paul Warner writes in an e-mail
message to me (April 30, 2010) "during the 50 years that I knew
him, I never heard [Robert] utter an unkind word about anyone."
Bob's commitment to the vocation of "book stewarding" could not
be thwarted. He found a way to . . . begin again.[3]

2. At the aforementioned SCM National Council meeting in Edmonton in
May of 1975, "there was no word of welcome or official recognition" of Bob
Miller and the others who had come with him; they were offered no help in
finding a place to stay; and they were treated throughout as "adversaries"—
almost as criminals. Had not Richard Allen (who attended the meeting at
his own expense) claimed the floor long enough to introduce Bob and his
supporters, the students and National Staff present would have been content
to ignore them altogether; they had already been 'informed' about them!
One can only imagine how this treatment must have pained Bob Miller.
(See *Statement and Observations Respecting the Book Store Issue at National
Council, 1975,* signed by Bob Miller, Carol Vine, Rose Fackenheim, in
association with Dick Allen and Fred Heiderich.)

3. The metaphor of 'beginning again' can only be appreciated by those who
have experienced the humiliations, frustrations and injustices of undeserved
failure and the courage required to "pick up the pieces" and try once more.
A paragraph from Paul Warner's e-mail message to me after he had read the
initial manuscript for this chapter conveys something of the anguish involved
in this sad affair for both himself and Bob.

"The book store episode elicited an anger in me that is as raw today as it was
then, changing my whole attitude towards money and people. It frightened
Robert at the time, and we never discussed it again. Money had never been
important to me. It became so that I was determined that never again would
I be placed in such a position.

"When we started to set up the new book store, the SCM group attempted a
smear campaign with the publishers trying to prevent us from buying books.

With the help of loyal friends, including some of the other employees of the SCM Book Room who left with him, Bob opened the Bob Miller Book Room in 1975 at a good location on Bloor Street. That was the year the Hall family moved to Montreal, and with all my new responsibilities at McGill there were few opportunities to visit Toronto. Montreal *was* still very much a bilingual Canadian city, despite Quebec's official unilingualism, and despite the victory of Rene Levesque's Parti Quebecois the year after our arrival (1976). Our French-speaking children soon felt very much at home, thus proving the truth of Bob's prediction that in a short while we would stop pining for "dear old Saskatoon" and be very glad that we had come to Montreal.

Two or three months after our arrival, two recently published books of mine began to issue in a number of invitations to speak—especially in the USA, where religious questions could command a great deal of interest still. Very often my trips on the lecture circuit over the next decades took me through, or sometimes to, Toronto; and while I never did become *very* familiar with the Bob Miller Book Room, I visited Bob there on several occasions. Clearly, it was a "different" sort of bookstore. For one thing, it was *quiet*. One could peruse the shelves for new books, or sit and read, or *just sit*—and listen to the beautiful music that was always there in the background, but never distractingly or loudly. I remember once walking into the book-filled space and hearing the wonderful voice of Kathleen Ferrier singing Handel: one could only stop and listen. No "helpful" clerks here, confronting customers with solicitous smiles and offers of instant service—though they were there if you needed them. The store always seemed to me like an extension

It didn't work. Robert mortgaged the Howland Avenue house to cover the loans from the Flessemans. I had the Mill evaluated and put it up for sale (the evaluation was $250,000; however, we needed the money quickly so I told the realtor to accept the first cash offer for $100,000, so it sold quickly. (The only time I had ever seen Robert weep). I also took a full time job apart from the work at the store and shared my income with Robert for three years until we, the owners, were able to take incomes . . . I didn't take a salary from the store until all the loans from people were repaid with interest" (e-mail communication, May 12, 2010).

of its owner and namesake. Usually I would wait until Bob could go out for lunch, or find a moment in his busy life for a brief chat.

2

In February of 1979, as I've mentioned earlier in another connection, the Canadian Theological Students' Conference was meeting in Montreal. Gregory Baum and I had been asked to speak. My lectures were later published by the Anglican Book Room in Toronto, with an introduction by Gregory, under the title, *The Canada Crisis*. It was the twenty-fifth anniversary of the annual Conference, which Bob had initiated in 1954. For that reason, and in the light of the upheaval over the SCM Book Room, Rhoda and I felt that it was high time that Bob Miller be recognized for this important accomplishment. The student committee charged with making local arrangements agreed, and accordingly invited Bob to appear at a reception at the Birks Building, which houses McGill's Faculty of Religious Studies, on the Sunday evening just prior to the weeklong deliberations of the conference. When he received this invitation from Stephen Hopkins, chair of the student planning committee, Bob wrote a typically tongue-in-cheek letter to me on the carbon copy of his response to Stephen:

> Dear Douglas: Since this nonsense is your doing, I am turning to Rhoda and you for accommodation. If you reject me, then surely the Allens or Desplands will take me in. [Dick and Nettie Allen and their sons were taking a sabbatic leave in Montreal that year and living quite near us. Sheila McDonough and her then-husband Michel Despland were also in the vicinity]. I'll need linguistic guidance also in that foreign country. Would it be possible to arrange a little gathering with the aforementioned on Saturday or Sunday so that I can visit with them all. I shall want to go around and visit with Mrs McDonough [Sheila's mother] also. And that will be it in Montreal. I won't have to spend long at the Conference, will I?—or do anything but bow?

Evelyn Reid was persuaded to come along with Bob, and I met them when they arrived at the Gare Centrale on Friday afternoon prior to the event. They were astonished at finding our house full of music—"a regular conservatory." Two of our children were on the way to becoming professional musicians, and while the house is a fairly spacious one, every room had multiple uses. Bob later reported to his mother back home that Christopher was even practicing (clarinet) in the main bathroom where there were good acoustics. ("Wonderful kids," he told her). As proposed, there was a party at our place that night, and it proved a happy occasion for all our old friends. The reception honouring Bob as founder of the Theological Students' Conference was held Sunday evening in the Junior Common Room of the Birks Building, with a hundred or more in attendance. Dick Allen, as I reported earlier, made an informative and appreciative speech, and Bob was asked to cut the large cake that was suitably lettered to fit the celebration. He didn't speak—I don't recall whether he bowed or not! But he did greet old McGill and other friends, and persons he had not met in recent years, like Allister and Millie McKinnon of the Philosophy Department, whom Rhoda had made sure were invited. Most of the students, who were present from across the country, did not know Bob; probably their only conception of him had filtered down, unfortunately, from the recent bookstore "scandal." But for those of us who knew him well it was at least a small occasion on which to express public gratitude for his work as study secretary of the SCM. Whether anyone meeting at forthcoming annual meetings of the Theological Students Conference, more than a quarter century later, will be aware that the organization was begun by Bob Miller (whether they will even connect it with the SCM!) remains in doubt. And I can hear Bob Miller saying, "It doesn't matter." Historical amnesia is "the name of the game" today. But a few of us know perfectly well that an ecumenical forum of Canadian theological students would have waited a good many years to emerge into view if it had depended on the theological colleges and educators and churches that supported them.

3

The Bob Miller Book Room became Bob's life until he retired at age seventy in 1989–1990. What Paul Warner calls Bob's "work ethic" was rigorous indeed: "He would often start work at six in the morning, [and] work through to seven at night. He always brought work to the Mill, the Island, or the farm when he came on weekends—which is why the business was a success."[4] He managed to get away occasionally to New York, where he would attend as many operas as possible, sometimes in the company of his cousin, Mary McInroy, of London, Ontario; and he retreated often to the farm that his friend Paul Warner had bought at Hillier, near Belleville, Ontario. Evelyn Reid lived with them there for a time. But the book room was Bob's primary concern. For him, it was not just a matter of stocking books and filling orders. He knew his books, and he knew his clientele and their needs. It was this reputation for knowledge of the world of books that prompted someone (actually, it was an employee of the giant business created by a onetime neighbour of ours in Montreal, Chapters) to say that the Bob Miller Book Room was the only real bookstore in Toronto. And in the *Toronto Globe and Mail* obituary that contained a wonderful photograph taken by Bob's longtime friend Imogene Walker, and headed "Bookseller Was a Spiritual Guide," Mr Damian Tarnopolsky wrote:

> Rev. Miller's breadth of knowledge, range of interests, and kind supportive attitude made him a guide to countless students whom he advised not only on texts and courses but on wider issues . . .
>
> Rev. Miller was a kind and private man but his seriousness of purpose could make him appear forbidding. Publishers' representatives quaked before seeing him and he was unwilling to suffer fools gladly, Ms [Carol] Vine recalled.[5]

Mr Tarnopolsky might have added professors and researchers to the list of those who consulted Bob Miller regularly—though

---

4. Paul Warner in an email message to me dated April 30, 2010.

5. *Toronto Globe and Mail* "Obituaries," February 9, 2003.

I know that Bob was disappointed that with a few exceptions, the theological colleges, including his own alma mater, Emmanuel, made so little use of his extraordinary stock and services.

There weren't many written communications from this period, but among the ones that I saved is a note about Gladys Miller's death (as so often, the note is undated, but it must have been some time in 1985): "My mother died this past weekend at 92. It wasn't the death that was sad, but the seven long years that had to lead up to it." Bob was very fond of his mother, and I know that it must have been terribly painful for him that, during her latter years, her memory left her—in the end, to the point that she didn't even know him. Prior to her illness, Mrs Miller always seemed to me an attractive and competent woman, a person of substance. Dick Allen, who knew her better than I since he lived at 105 Howland on two separate occasions, writes, "She certainly knew her own mind and could be decisive when needed, but she had a wonderful sense of humour that enlivened the dinner table and rode over moments of awkwardness. She was most accommodating to the passing parade of students, was a kind of house mother, in whose second floor bed-sitting room all gathered Sunday evenings for that dreadful Ed Sullivan show! If Bob got anything from her, it was the lively humour that broke through the reserve from time to time and lifted everyone's spirits."[6] She was, I think, extremely proud of her elder son, and was glad in retirement to live her own life in his orbit—though perhaps she may often have wondered about his decisions and about some of the people around him. Bob's devotion to her was evident to all who knew him, and he expected those who professed friendship towards him to honour her, even in her later years. I think his feeling for his mother informed his relationship with women, and especially mothers, generally. In several of his post-retirement letters and notes to me, he expresses concern about *my* mother, whom he had met on several occasions, some of them, like Dad's funeral and our wedding, highly memorable ones. "I hope your 'old mum' is still in reasonable shape—as reasonable as one can expect at that age." . . . "Greetings to Doug's

6. Email message to me dated May 28, 2010.

mother. Hope she's healthy to 100!" (In fact, when she died in 2005 she was five months short of a hundred, and had outlived Bob by two years.) His attitude towards his mother—and other peoples' mothers—was part of that deep *pastoral* sense that, quoting Evelyn Reid and others, I have mentioned in previous pages. While Bob could be brusque with sales representatives and pretentious academics and other self-important persons, he always demonstrated a surprisingly warm and humble demeanour in the presence of those whose health, age (whether old or very young), family circumstances or other particulars made them vulnerable to life or precluded affectation of any sort.

During the 1980s, Bob Miller found more and more pleasure, meaning and, perhaps, solace in the contemplation of works of art. Western art had become newly fascinating to him during his sojourn in Europe, but now, increasingly, he turned to the art of the Orient. I remember an evening in the 'eighties when he took Rhoda and me to his small room at 105 Howland Avenue and showed us print after print of Japanese paintings, scrolls and calligraphy. One could not mistake his excitement at discovering all that hidden treasure. Later he wrote to Rhoda,

> I am going to N.Y. at the end of November when both Sotheby's and Christies have their big annual auction of Chinese painted scrolls. It's not that I'll buy anything, but for 3 or 4 days paintings are hanging in several large rooms for inspection, and it is the most wonderful way to see the real thing in real life. It is like a huge specialized art gallery. You can also sit at a table and ask to see the hand scrolls, and they are brought to you to unfold and pore over at will. It's like being handed a Matisse or a Rembrandt or whoever to inspect at close quarters.

He was writing from "the farm" he shared with Paul and Evelyn. "You should have been stopping over here at the farm on your way to Montreal. Evelyn just arrived here yesterday from her summer at the River [her summer place on the Crowe River], so she is done in from closing up there and from construction-work she is engaged in there ... Emil [Fackenheim] was here a couple of weeks ago and all seems well with them. Susie and her new husband are living in England for three years so he won't have to be drafted into the Israeli army. Rose doesn't travel with Emil but stays with Joshi, who doesn't take easily to either of them going away . . .".

A little later there was a letter telling us that Ellen Flesseman's granddaughter, a student of medicine in Amsterdam, planned to spend "a two-month stint of some kind with a doctor in Montreal," and he remarks, "My life goes its uneventful way. We have received our first order for the 3 volumes of Prof. Hall's contextual theology! We don't see Evelyn much anymore—were supposed to go there for New Year's but I had the flu or some such affliction. Some day I have hopes of getting out of the book business, but I don't know when or how. Bob."

In 1989–1990, Rhoda and I had a remarkable sabbatical year. In Japan, where I was visiting scholar at Doshisha University in Kyoto, we had front-row seats, so to speak, on the traumatic and tragic events in Tianenmen Square in Bejing; then we went to our old European haunt of Münster in Westphalia where we had front-row seats on the great changes (*die Wende*) that signaled the end of the East/West division of Germany and of the cold war. Bob mailed his letter of September 14th, 1989, to our Montreal address—

> I am writing this on the assumption that it will be in a cupboard somewhere until you return to Montreal a year hence—or maybe it will be sent to you unless you have been sent home because no-one is left in East Germany! I guess it is all in the interests of a reunited Germany—in any case, or all cases, it won't matter. I have been so deluged with mail from you—lovely postcards to put up on my display shelf—though nothing lovely about the old BMBR [Bob Miller Book Room] postcard which Rhoda used.
>
> You must have been on the underside of Japan—the George Grant side?[7] I am sending your memorial[8] on to John Coleman, with whom I first met George Grant on a long walk along the Humber. The Colemans will share it with Evelyn.

7. We're puzzled by this reference, but it is somehow connected with the fact that—*from Japan*—Rhoda had sent Bob a copy of the "memorial piece" that she had written for our friend George Grant.

8. The above.

We are deluged with the beginning of university, except in the theology department. *The T.S.T. seems to mostly go elsewhere for their books. So a decent theological book store is obviously of no interest to them.* [my italics]. But I won't be around for that much longer anyway, and that part of the business will fade out . . . I still indulge myself in orientalia—and it is indulgence. Bob.

4

In 1990 Bob transferred the ownership of the Bob Miller Book Room to Carol Vine, a faithful friend and helper throughout the turbulent final days of the SCM Book Room. Carol told me very recently that it is flourishing still. In 1991 he and Paul left, earlier than they had planned, for the West Coast, where they intended to retire.[9] They made a brief visit with cousin Mary McInroy in London which, as their correspondence shows, all three enjoyed immensely. That summer Bob wrote to us from the house they had bought in Victoria on Somass Drive. The letter contained some unhappy news:

My intentions of visiting old friends in the east in May and June were cut short because I couldn't any longer take the unsettled life and living in empty rooms with packed boxes, so Paul and I took off on our final western journey. It's not a case of young men going west any more.

Last week we had visits from Evelyn Reid and Rose and Emil Fackenheim. Rose is very ill with what some doctors say is early Alzheimers, and others say is definitely not but don't know what. It is very, very sad. Emil carries on with their lives and his work in a marvellous way and it was wonderful having them here.

9. "I asked Bob to come and share my home in Victoria when he retired . . . His spare time was spent in building an Asian Art Collection . . . Researching the paintings and reading the books required to build the collection gave him great pleasure" (Paul Warner, in an e-mail message to me dated April 30, 2010).

105 Howland has been sold to Peter Reid and his wife and their two small children.

Tama [Copithorne] lives in Vanc [Vancouver] and Evelyn was going to visit with her this week. I haven't seen her, nor Margaret Prang

I hope your multiple families are thriving and being musically productive and that you are both well and enjoying life and work—and being Canadian. Bob

As this note indicates, Bob already had several very good friends in Vancouver and Victoria, and as it turned out a number of them were good friends of Rhoda's and mine, too. Sometime in 1992 [the letters were still dateless, in many cases] he wrote to "Dear Rhoda (and Doug too): "Your letter could not have been better timed. We had a weekend with Mary Bailey and her sister Helen, from White Rock. Helen has been a close friend . . . since we were in the same class at Victoria. I have known Mary since she and Helen ran their place in Port Carling . . ."

Then the letter goes on—to our considerable amusement—to speak about Mary (Marshall) Bailey's grandchildren, the children of Mary Lou and Stan Day, our closest family friends for years in Saskatoon. Probably we had never talked with Bob about them. Mary, a professional psychiatrist and wife of the late head of medical faculty at the University of Saskatchewan, was a very good friend too, and Stephen Day, her grandson, was our godchild. Canada is a small place, population wise, and one is always discovering hidden relationships of this sort. He goes on—

Evelyn was also here when Rose and Emil came to visit. It was very sad to be with Rose without her old sparkle, and to realize how hard it is for Emil when he should now be having someone look after him . . .

Ellen [Flesseman] died in June 1991. She had cancer of the larynx for the last three years. I spent the last three Christmasses there with her and her family. She had always said she wanted to decide when her life should end and not drag on with her condition. Her son-in-law is a doctor and when the time came he helped her.

My life here is completely irrelevant and I am enjoying it immensely and not bothered by the irrelevancy . . . I can't imagine it better. Hope Doug's book is progressing. Bob

The "irrelevancy" he almost boasts of here consisted in some measure of his ability to notice and enjoy (at last!—one could almost say) the world of nature. "We have beautiful sunshine, blue sky and fresh, fresh air. I am sitting in front of the window in my room looking over the back gardens to the Straits of Juan de Fuca. Boats are moored in the bay and beyond—nothing but the deep blue sea. The house is beautiful, the city is beautiful, life is beautiful."[10]

This deep satisfaction with "life" is sounded again in another letter of the period: "There is a gull's nest on the roof across from us, nicely built in a corner sheltered from the wind but not from the rain, which is pouring down today. The nest and the mother will be a soaking mess. The father flies in regularly, presumably to bring her something to eat. Occasionally, she leaves the nest bare and sits upon the nearby ledge."[11]

The only other time I can recall Bob's love of nature was his obvious enjoyment of the Georgian Bay country where we first met; but I know that this feeling for the natural order, which relates to his appreciation of solitude, was deep seated. Like many of us—perhaps in some ways like all of us!—I think that he missed that world during the busy, city- and people-dominated years of his working life.

Bob had experienced some serious health problems (prostate cancer) by 1994 and had spent some time in Seattle when there were too many demands on the British Columbia health system to deal with his case. There was a new and noticeable jerkiness in his penmanship when he wrote in the fall of that year:[12]

10. From a letter to Mary McInroy from 2713 Somass Drive in Victoria—undated, as usual.

11. From an undated letter to Mary McInroy.

12. To Mary McInroy he wrote, about this time, "I have become fed up

I've been back in Victoria since the end of August and time has gone as fast—or maybe it doesn't go at all, it just *is*—as in heaven. The last month in Seattle and the first couple here were pretty uncomfortable but now all the effects of the treatment have passed and I eat and sleep and walk and visit and rebuild an old relic for use a little longer yet. Whether the treatment actually worked has yet to be discovered. As you can see, I have some difficulty with a trembling hand—its extent varies and hopefully will decrease with time. We have numerous eastern visitors since my return and have talked with Evelyn Reid and John Coleman and yesterday with Mary Bailey, who had had a fine visit with her sister in Muskoka and then a month with [her daughter] Helen and John in Seattle (whom I got to know and appreciate a little—i.e., know a little and appreciate much!

Hope all continues well with your children (your grown-ups!) and their musical pursuits, and that your book progresses with élan. . . Thanks for your letters and concerns.

Another letter later that year ventured into the knotty question of Quebec independence—seen from the perspective of "the West Coast":

Sorry I did not have my letter awaiting your return from the is-land [our summer place in the North Channel of Lake Huron]. And if I don't get it away this week the postage rates in Quebec will likely go up! I have to say I think the general reaction [to Quebec's separation from Canada] would be great relief . . . , but it will of course be such a difficult upheaval, and of course it is going to cost every one of us a considerable sum of money. We are all going to be carried away in the American corporate melting pot anyway, and fragmentation will not protect anyone but only speed the process.

I guess I had written to him about my study—my monk's cell!—in our basement, in the former built-in garage that my

---

with this shaking and just yesterday the doctor started me on something called Sinemet. You may remember years ago I had a painful, stiff knee. I even remember that it was especially bad the night we were in Massey Hall to hear *Eugene Onegin* . . . What could be more obscene than this writing!" (undated postcard).

nephew Rick had helped me transform into what I thought a very cozy place in which to write. "If your theology comes out of the basement," Bob asks puckishly, does that make it an underground document?" He had just finished reading our mutual friend Margaret Prang's book *A Heart at Leisure from Itself: Caroline Macdonald of Japan*.[13] "It is amazing," he commented, "how such an important and well-known and respected person could disappear so completely. Maybe history is just so much baggage that we are better off without."

There was another puckish letter sometime before Christmas in 1995:

> Dear Rhoda and Doug,
>
> You will recognize these scenes [in the margins of the paper] from our bucolic Western life. We are joining a movement to separate from all that lies beyond the mountains. We are fed up with the antics of you people over there—*whatever* language you speak. You will need your passport for your next visit here . . . –Bob and Paul.

The next note, still in December of '95, enclosed a *Globe and Mail* article on palliative care written by our mutual friend Hilda Powicke, in which Hilda speaks of her volunteer work at Toronto's Mount Sinai Hospital. Bob notes, "Hilda seems still to be very much on the go.

> I sent a copy to Evelyn, who reported enthusiastically on her visit with you in Montreal. Also to Margaret Prang in Vancouver, whom I discover in her Christmas letter had a stroke in November which affected her left side seriously—though now she seems to be much on the mend and is taking it as a very good warning.
>
> We have been reading *How we Die* by S. B. Noland, which is certainly a plain statement of what is ahead for many of us."

A year later there was a brief note that takes up the theme of human limitations. Referring to a poem of Robert Frost's, Bob

---

13. Margaret Prang, *A Heart at Leisure from Itself: Caroline McDonald of Japan* (Vancouver: UBC Press, 1995).

notes that human beings can neither see very far nor understand very deeply; but like Frost he concludes that even the knowledge of such confining limits to our strivings should never prevent us from making the effort.

That letter closes with what I recognized as a paraphrase of the final words of Samuel Becket's 1955 novel, *The Unnamable*— three short sentences that express rather precisely the human situation as Bob Miller, in his bleaker moments, now perceived it:

Just go on. We go on.
We cannot go on.
Well, we go on

But then his faith found the wherewithal to counter his bleakness with three words that did not come from Becket's pen: "*And praise be!*" Old and sick and "irrelevant as he felt he was, and knowing better than most how terribly difficult it is to "go on," Bob Miller was still ready to affirm the human journey, and to praise its Source.

In the fall of 1997, I had to give some lectures at Holden Village, the innovative and influential retreat centre of the Evangelical Lutheran Church of America located high in the Cascade Mountains of Washington State. Afterwards, Rhoda and I flew to Vancouver to visit with friends there. Bob had written that he would like to come across from Victoria for an extended visit with us. He took us to dinner with a number of old friends, and in the evening we had a lovely supper with Margaret Prang and her friend Maria Fuerstenwald in their apartment. Later Bob wrote that the day in Vancouver "was very enjoyable," though it seemed to us that he did not look at all well. After we had gone, he and his friend Joyce Searcy had attended the final opera production of the Victoria company—*Carmen*. "The Carmen," he wrote, "was a young soprano from Nova Scotia singing her first *Carmen*. She tried hard but was obviously a nice young woman from Nova Scotia, and Carmen's seductiveness and oomph was just not in her genes or bones or wherever it is supposed to be. The tenor lost his voice as soon as he arrived and another had to be flown in at the last minute. The singing tenor stood down in the orchestra and the voiceless tenor acted and mouthed the part on stage. It was not the most successful of productions. We have our troubles."

The same letter comments on British Columbia politics:

We are now in the midst of our provincial election with a selection of unappetizing leaders to choose from. The separatist party doesn't seem to be running in our riding so I am either voting Green or purposely destroying my ballot. I am not voting N.D.P., Liberal or Reform. I don't know whether I shall confess this to Dick Allen.

5

Early in 1998, my old friends Jim and Alma (Martin) Ireland sent me some old pictures they had discovered among their souvenirs: Beausoleil Island and our memorable time there fifty years earlier. We were all so young! I sent them on to Bob, and he wrote: "Thanks for the memories of lazy afternoons, dreamy soft lagoons . . . Sorry McCleary isn't somewhere visible. I have sent the sheet of photos on to Olwen [Anderson]. She will recognize even more people than I do. I have enclosed her letter for you to read the piece on the back about her going to school—Northern Tech."

I was pleased to see that Bob's memories of that summer, and of the quite unusual young peoples' group from WoodGreen Church during the ministry of the remarkable Ray McCleary, were as fond as mine. That Tom Thompson country of Georgian Bay leaves indelible pictures on the mind, and people like Olwen Anderson, with whom Bob corresponded quite regularly until her death, represented the very best of post-war youth. Its like, I suspect, cannot be found today. Olwen is mentioned in a later letter, too—one written in June of 1999. She had sent him a copy of a talk she had given about the Queen-St./Broadview area in "the old days" in Toronto.

But his great news in that letter was that "I have been given a ticket to Tokyo, and am off in two days for 7-10 days. 'Tokyo, Kyoto and Nara'—that's our itinerary. My Japanese friend from

Toronto is coming with me." Knowing of Rhoda's and my interest in Japan, he was glad to share this news with us. But I think the trip proved too strenuous—and much too short—for him. On his return, he wrote: "I don't really have any impression of Japan. Only of several temples, many sculptures and paintings. It was all somewhat overwhelming—3 days in Tokyo, 4 in Koyto, 1 in Nara and in Kamakura and [indecipherable]. National Museums in the first 3 cities. Antique districts and shops and malls. I came home with half a dozen small paintings. To properly take in what we saw would need about 6 weeks, the Japanese language, and a pocketful of money—and of course we hardly really *saw* anything of the treasures that are all around to see" [August 1999].

Bob's collection of "Orientalia" had by this time grown to attract the attention of the Art Gallery in Victoria, and in the Spring of 1999 they had mounted a display of some of his treasures. "The gallery has no money for such," he wrote, "in fact for nothing other than the preservation of itself. This was one of the ways of putting on a show with no outlay. My Japanese friend came from Toronto and photographed it all. I sent Evelyn a set for perusal. She suggested keeping it for a month longer so that you could see it when you stop over." This, however, did not materialize. Our visit at that time was too short. When Mary McInroy visited him in Victoria, Bob took her to the gallery where, Mary writes, "he was warmly welcomed."

Bob's handwriting was becoming increasingly shaky. We had to puzzle sometimes over a letter that arrived late in the summer of 2002. We had just returned to Montreal from our little paradise in the North Channel of Lake Huron—half an acre on tiny Mitchell Island off Algoma Mills, where we'd spent most of our summers since we had acquired the property at the end of our memorable parish life in nearby Blind River. Our four children still regard it as their real home, and now, with their own families, summers at Spendthrift, as we call our place, are not the quiet retreat they once were when we were only six. Unfortunately, Bob never visited us there, but he had a mental image of the place from all our letters and conversation about it. He wrote, "With all your family around at various times I well imagine that you had a rambunctious time and likely needed to get home for a rest. But it is wonderful to be able to have them around, and to have a wonderful fun place to be with them."

The main subject of that letter, however, concerned our great friend, Leslie Peterson, who had just retired in London, Ontario, after years in Sault Ste Marie as bishop of Algoma, one of the largest Anglican dioceses in Canada. Les and his wife, Yvonne, had both been loyal and active members of the Student Christian Movement at the University of Western Ontario, and when Rhoda and I were at St Andrew's United Church in Blind River they were at the Anglican parish in nearby Eliot Lake, so we had many happy visits with them and their five children. Les and I had actually driven down to the University of Chicago in 1962 to hear Karl Barth's American lectures at the Rockefeller Chapel. Barth offered five lectures and several appearances with a panel of American theologians. Jaroslav Pelikan chaired the panels, and Bill Stringfellow, whom Barth later called the most interesting theologian in the USA, was on it. We met Barth after his final lecture. He went on to Princeton from Chicago, and spent one night at Union Seminary in a fascinating discussion with John Bennett, William Pauck, and others. Pauck, who once described Barth as "a friendly bear," kept insisting, in the discussion, that Barth was really "a Platonist"—or so I was told by an Australian friend who was present. It was the great theologian's only visit to North America. The lectures were published later under the title *Evangelical Theology*.

"My cousin Mary McInroy who lives in London," Bob wrote, "phoned to tell me about Les's death, and sent me the two enclosures. I thought I should save them for you in case you were in the Malucco Islands or some other such place!" Bob had come to know Les Peterson during his visits to Western as study secretary, and I know that he recognized in this extraordinary man what always endeared him to so many of us. Les Peterson was the most *guileless* human being I have ever known, and one of the most authentically Christian. Like Bob, he too was "quiet" in a certain "Kierkegaardian" way, but unlike Bob he showed one a good deal about what was going on in his mind and heart. I know that the two quite liked and respected one another. Les had visited Bob in Victoria that summer. He was only back from the trip west for a day or so when he died very suddenly. He was just seventy-three years of age

Other old friends are mentioned in this same rather nostalgic letter. Marie-Jeanne Coleman had had a small heart attack: "I called John today, and M-J answered the phone. She is home resting and hopes to have learned to take life more easily." Gwen Grant, the wife of John Grant, the Canadian church historian who taught at Emmanuel College for many years, had died. Dick Allen "had a prostate operation, and they hope the results will be positive." There were visits from Carol Vine and her son, Imogene Walker, Margaret Norman, and two of Bob's cousins. Paul had found an article about George Grant in the paper "and said I should send it along to Doug because of his interest in George. You can see how well I have saved it!"

"Keep well and enjoy the time that is left," he concluded. Then, reminding us of one of his favourite Auden poems, he added a characteristic caveat: we are all of course victims of Time—which is "indifferent in a week to a beautiful physique"; nevertheless we may hope to acquire, for "the time that is left," enough courage to enjoy the life and the work that has been given us.

6

I had to give lectures for a week in July of 2003 at the Pacific Lutheran University in Tacoma, Washington, so Rhoda and I made it an occasion to visit our friends on the West Coast, of whom there were now several. We saved our visit with Bob until near the end of our sojourn "out there." The resourceful Paul Warner had acquired for them a fabulous house on Wildflower Lane in Victoria. We followed Bob's instructions and made our way in our rented car up the hill on which this modern mansion was located—only to notice Bob, thin and beautifully attired in a suit that was just a little out of date, coming down the hill to meet us. He was obviously not very well, but greeted us with his usual infectious smile. The house was a virtual museum! Paul's taste in furnishings had always intrigued us, and this was his ultimate triumph. He served from the kitchen while Bob and Rhoda and I sat in great style at a beautiful antique table and were treated to the most delicious brunch ever. At one point, we spoke about one of our revered old teachers, John Coleman Bennett, who had been President of Union Seminary in the difficult years of the student upheavals, and was the great encourager and champion of my books. I had corresponded with Dr Bennett for many years, and visited him and Anne on several occasions. During my last visit (Rhoda was with me too, that time) my old friend, really another father-figure for me, was nearly ninety-five and ill. "He could hardly finish a sentence," I told Bob. "He would dissolve into tears and have to stop talking . . ."

"Yes," Bob said, "there's that." It was a revealing remark.

We drove down to a favorite restaurant of theirs for dinner, and later while Rhoda and Paul chatted at one end of the large living room, Bob and I sat in a friendly silence for some time, interspersed with short exchanges that were, I felt, overlaid with the knowledge that this could well be our last conversation. Looking about the luxurious room and remembering the astonishing collection of oriental art Bob had shown us earlier, I found myself asking him, "Do you feel sometimes that those days of yore—your time with the SCM, your Book Room—were almost another life altogether?"

"Yes," he said.

I suppose we might have gone on from there—and for a long time. But somehow that yes said it all. After a prolonged pause, I looked across the room where he sat in profile, looking old and weary. And again a question took hold of me that I couldn't suppress: "Do you feel that you have had a happy life?" It was an impertinence, really—but it came out all by itself.

Bob didn't take it as an impertinence, though. He let it simmer for at least a full minute, and then he answered in the way that I expected he would answer: "Yes—I suppose so."

It was indeed our last visit, as it turned out. But there was an important aftermath. Back on *our* island in Lake Huron that

August, I wrote a short note to Bob, thanking him and telling him of our return to the less dramatic forests of northern Ontario. But the real purpose of my note was to express my deep gratitude for all that he had given me, and meant to me.

> Sincere thanks, dear old friend, for receiving us so warmly—like the Prodigal Son's father, coming way down the road to meet us! I wish we could sit and chat for days on end (with, of course, the appropriate long silences), so that all the shyness and hesitation would vanish. You see, you are still a kind of hero for me—or at least an elder and more sophisticated brother. But perhaps heaven, if such there be, will prove the kind of place where the likes of us can sit on the grass and discourse in utter freedom and openness. Meanwhile, the few hours with you were wonderfully reassuring for two simple Canadian souls who love and respect you deeply.[14]

Bob's response—his last letter to us—is undoubtedly one of the most poignant of all his communications over the years. At least it is that to me.

> And Douglas, such a letter to write! And thank you for it.
>
> I hope you shall again be summoned to the West Coast of the continent and that you will include a drop-off with us—maybe a little longer.
>
> For example, I didn't want to get started talking about some of the things that were around us downstairs [the art, the furnishings] because it could go on and on, and there were so many other things to talk about. It was more important to acquire a little sense of where we were in our lives—and that of course includes families and friends . . .
>
> We talked about the political orientation of many of the people you meet on your travels, because that is so much on all our minds: the USA now. But that is really a secondary matter. I was sorry afterward not to have asked you about the reason you are doing all this [travels on the lecture circuit, books, etc.]—about what you look for and what you find, what you feel you have to contribute. *We did not get to the centre of it all.* Well, on

14. 30 July 2003.

> a hot Saturday afternoon, with so many other important things
> to talk about, and just to be—together.
>
> Recently the *Globe and Mail* had a special section devoted
> to summer camps for children, and there was a whole page on
> Beausoleil Island in Ontario, with a picture. I was reminded of
> the WoodGreen camp we all went to there. It was just before I
> went overseas . . .

Rhoda had sent him a copy of the 'citation' that had been read
out at the ceremony in Rideau Hall in October, when the Gover-
nor General Adrienne Clarkson had pinned an Order of Canada
medal on me. The remarkable General Romeo Dallaire was made
a Companion of the Order that day, and we had a memorable conversation with him and Mme Dallaire. It was a wonderful occasion
for me and my family—and especially because I'd been given the
honour because of my work as a *Protestant theologian*. We felt it
was a recognition of an aspect of Canadian history that has been
rather unrecognized, especially in recent years. We were proud to
be able to share this with our old friend, and I know that he was
proud too.

But Bob thought the citation ought to have gone farther!
"It should have included a more regal statement of the classical
Protestant intellectual tradition. We need to be reminded that our
forefathers include Luther, Calvin, Knox, Erasmus, Kierkegaard,
Barth—and not just Aquinas and Augustine and John Paul II."

The letter ended with what I heard as a final reiteration of
the message that Robert W. Miller had conveyed to me at the beginning and all along the way—oddly enough in almost the same
words Adrienne Clarkson whispered as she placed the "snowflake"
medal on my lapel: "Keep at it as long as the both of you can take it
and that it gives you satisfaction—yes, even pleasure."

A month or so later—on November 11th—Bob telephoned
us to say that his doctors had given him six months to a year to
live. He wanted to let us know himself, he said. It was not surprising news, really, but it was . . . sad. Very sad. "*Time that is intolerant
of the brave and innocent, and indifferent in a week to a beautiful
physique . . .*" (Auden).

He wasn't given the "six months to a year" the medics promised.

At the beginning of December in 2003, I was attending a conference in Namibia. The United Nations (UN) AIDS committee, quite surprisingly, invited some twenty-five or thirty theologians from around the world to attend a meeting in that beautiful, sorrowful land, the former German South West Africa, to try to get at the roots of the prejudice against and stigmatization of persons with AIDS. Among the reasons for such prejudice and stigmatization, *religion* was probably at the top of the list.

We met at a marvelous conference centre in the hills not far from the charming little capital city, Windhoek—"the hook of the wind." With its Lutheran churches and its neat shops, Windhoek is like a nineteenth century German town, transplanted into the rolling deserts of Africa. And all around, especially in the northern part of Namibia, AIDS conducts its ghastly assault on the poor vulnerable people. In some places, the people were so weary digging graves for the victims that the graves, we were told, became shallower and shallower: the poor diggers, most of them victims of HIV/AIDS themselves, just didn't have the strength to go deeper.

The conference was full of interest for me, and of promise. It was the first time that theologians had been bidden by the UN to see what they could come up with out of the two-thousand year history of *our* religion to combat the inhuman, nearly inconceivable stigmatization of people with HIV and AIDS, far too much of it inspired by some horrendous but powerful version or versions of Christianity! From Africans, particularly, we heard stories of stigmatization, prejudice and outright banishment that made the blood run cold.

Despite its promise, however, I found the conference disappointing. Many of the 'theologians' present were in fact not theologians, but persons loosely connected with the various churches. I sensed immediately that one of the primary reasons why 'Christians' could contribute so much vehemence to the rejection of AIDS victims was that for so many of them Christianity consisted of a compassionless moralism, with sexual 'sins' at the top of the list. One young Caucasian Anglican priest from South Africa, himself a victim of AIDS, had worked out a formula to explain the connections: AIDS = SEX = SIN = DEATH. When, in discussion, I tried to introduce the concept of sin as broken relationship, alienation, estrangement, I found that the idea was so utterly new to my fellow 'theologians' that they scarcely understood what I was talking about. Sin as bad behaviour and evil deed was so entrenched that even among the educated the *relational* conception of sin that belongs to the biblical and best traditional teaching of the church seemed a foreign language. So apparently was the indelible connection between sin and sex. When such ideas had such a hold on even the 'elite' among the Christians, why would anyone be surprised that it ended in the stigmatization of HIV-AIDS sufferers on the part of 'ordinary' Christians? The discussion was also stymied by an over-representation of a certain kind of Roman Catholicism. Whenever the word 'condom' was mentioned by some unsuspecting Lutheran or Presbyterian, there would be an immediate reaction from that contingent. The way to AIDS prevention, they insisted, lay in marital faithfulness and sexual restraint. Period. Try telling that to the workers uprooted from their rural settings and, in order to make a living, set down in cities far away from their families!

When the conference was over, I went with a few others whose flights were not taking off for a day or two, into Windhoek. After purchasing some trinkets for home, and some postcards, I sat down at one of the bright open-air cafes on a promenade near the centre, ordered coffee, and looked over the post-cards I'd chosen. There was a beautiful photograph of sand-dunes and hills by Gerald Hoberman, called "Sossusvlei." It reminded me of Antoine de Saint-Exupery's *Wind, Sand and Stars*—one of the very first books Bob Miller had insisted I should read.

"Why?" I had asked him way back then.

"Well, it's just beautiful prose," he said. And it is. It is also, of course, prose written by a man who, a little like Camus, seemed to me a little like Bob Miller, too!

So I wrote my first card from the bottom of Africa to Bob, who since his November 11th phone call was never far from my mind. I told him that the picture brought *Wind, Sand and Stars* immediately to mind, a book "to which you first introduced me— as you introduced me to much else besides.

> How grateful I feel for your life—for the gift of self-acceptance and the vocational direction you gave me. Dear friend of 55 years, I hope you are able to take pleasure sometimes from the memory of your good and generous life. I hope the pain is not too great, and that you are at peace. What a great mystery our human existence is!"

I know exactly what I wrote in that little café on December 12, 2003—because the card was never sent. I have it right here, in front of me.

After writing it, I thought I'd go to an Internet café I had discovered a few days earlier and see whether I could pick up my messages from cyberspace. The first message that popped onto the screen was from Evelyn Reid: "Bob Miller died this morning at 1:15." It had been sent from Evelyn's home in Niagara-on-the-Lake the day before: December 11th.

The next message was also from Evelyn, and was dated: 2003/12/10 Wed. AM 12:42 EST: It read:

> I talked tonight to Paul and Bob. Bob seems to be going down hill quite quickly. Paul thinks he may have had a couple of strokes. He is now in a wheelchair. For a few days he seemed to be struggling to keep his mind clear; cannot walk, is now in a bedroom on the same floor as Paul. Tonight they were enjoying a Hayden quartet and a Beethoven trio. They have had a lot of company this week . . . I asked if he is eating well, and he told me of one of their local friends who brings blue cheese one day, chocolate cake the next, cheese cake the day after. All of which he enjoys to a certain degree. He has to be nudged sometimes to eat. He is not able to read any more except the big headlines in newspapers. He tires quickly. Today he was quite clear in his thinking. Paul is domestically very capable, and Bob said tonight that he was quite comfortable, and I'm sure that is true.

Of course I'd known it was coming. One sensed that already in the summer, despite his attempt at a jaunty walk down that hill. But when one hears "six months to a year" one automatically chooses the date furthest away; and it was only a month—*exactly a month*—since we had received that phone call.

It was a very strange experience for me, hearing *such* news at *such* a distance! I looked around for a friend I had made at the conference—a Norwegian, Jan-Bjarne Sodal, who in some ways rather reminded me of Bob. He had already left for Johannesburg. So I had to absorb the news, and mourn, all alone and in a place far removed from . . . Beausoleil Island! There was no one with whom to talk about it until I reached Vienna days later, where I rejoined my dear Rhoda, who was visiting our Lucy there. We could mourn together—and remember, with true gratitude, our friend.

8

Bob Miller didn't wish to have a memorial service, but that should not convey to anyone the idea that he no longer considered himself a person of faith. A little while before his death, Bob composed his own obituary—just a couple of sentences:

> Miller, The Rev. Robert Whiteley—In his 84th year. He was active with the United Church of Canada, the Student Christian Movement, the S.C.M. Book Room, and the Bob Miller Book Room. He is survived by the four families of his brother Douglas. He has been supported by many of the choicest friends and his companion of 50 years, Paul Warner."
>
> Bob's ashes, Paul wrote, "are under a pear tree in the garden . . . "

Back home in Montreal after a month with our daughters in Vienna and Provence, I wrote a little memorial statement for Bob, which I sent to a few mutual friends with a personal addendum: "I do not know what my life might have been had Bob Miller not entered it. It would certainly not have been what it has been, the life of an itinerant theologian and seeker after understanding—*fides quarens intellectum.*"

4

A Life in Time

1

THE LIVES OF INDIVIDUALS are always affected by the spirit of the times in which they live, but some periods of history are especially determinative for individual destiny. 'The Sixties' constitute, in my view, such a period. More profoundly, I think, than the roaring Twenties, or the "dirty thirties," or even the warring forties, the approximately fifteen-year period beginning with the year 1960 introduced social and cultural conditions that exercised subtle influences upon the lives of individuals in both North America and Western Europe. These conditions were all the more decisive because, while producing some notable external manifestations, they were basically internal—fundamental changes of attitude, expectation and valuation, which rather quickly permeated every social institution and affected nearly every individual, whether those who were exuberantly animated by the cultural whirlwind, those who resented and resisted it, or those who were simply confused. The *Geist* of this period was greater than all of its *dramatis personae.* Viewed from the distance of half a century, one suspects that we were all, in Shakespeare's words, "merely players." Even those who thought themselves, or were perceived by others, as being principal *agents* of change, and therefore believed themselves to be exercising their personal freedom more heroically than ever before, in hindsight can be understood more accurately as vehicles and pawns of trends, fashions and ideologies that vastly transcended their personal wills and acts. Whether such currents of opinion took the form of vaguely Marxist visions, or assumed even vaguer bohemian countercultural lifestyles, or attempted odd and baffling combinations of the two, they were like tidal waves that swept up whole populations—and more especially persons, groups, and institutions inadequately anchored in traditions of critical vigilance and wisdom: in short, they swayed especially the young.

That is why these controlling currents of social change were most conspicuous among colonies of young people on the verge of maturity and craving purpose, recognition and power—that is to say: universities. The universities and colleges of North America and Western Europe became battlegrounds (sometimes quite literally) between the established authorities who naturally resisted radical change and coalitions of young discontented or visionary seekers after a new order. Inspired by "radical" professors and others who, sometimes for noble ideals and sometimes for less honourable motives, aspired to give shape and direction to the amorphous element of protest, millions of university students rose up against 'the Establishment' in the name of the New, liberation, justice, peace, democracy, freedom, "the greening of America," and other stirring and apparently virtuous causes. It was very heady stuff!

I do not say this as an outsider. I was by no means immune from the excitement of the hour. I too let my hair grow, cultivated a beard, and dressed in ways that shocked or amused my elders and superiors. I was inspired by Theodore Roszak's *The Making of a Counterculture* and other testaments of the dawning new age. As a teacher of Christian theology, I developed a whole course entitled 'Christ and the Counterculture,' which I offered not only as an elective at St. Andrew's College in the University of Saskatchewan but carried about on the lecture circuit for a time. I listened with enthusiasm to the "rock opera" *Jesus Christ Superstar* and other artistic expressions of countercultural fervor. I left my office door open to my students nearly all the time and spent literally hours, for almost a decade of my life, listening to the woes and enthusiasms of the young—and therefore I published very little before my forty-fifth year. I initiated or had membership in several interminable curricular revisions designed to make subject matter ever more accessible ("relevant") to students and, more important still, to give them a "say" in every aspect of their programs, including the assessment of their own work. Though it obviously detracted from any serious scholarly work or research, I approved of the insistence of students that they should have direct representation on every board, committee, or planning session—a pattern which of course entailed, throughout our universities at large, an exponential growth in administrative and committee work and made the administrative component of educational institutions, once regarded as a (relatively small!) enabling element, by far more significant than either teaching or research.

I also walked in peace marches, joined protests against Vietnam and violence, participated in sit-ins, wrote letters and signed petitions to officials, served on a committee to receive US draft-dodgers, etc., etc. I did not, it is true, give up lecturing in favor of spontaneous discourse with my classes—and I suffered for this, not only at the hands of some of my students but also in minds of some of my more "with-it" colleagues, who were happy to adopt the "what-shall-we-talk-about-today?" model of teaching that became popular in the sixties in all those disciplines that didn't actually require the transmission of *knowledge*. Emil Fackenheim told me that he just continued to lecture away on Hegel (his speciality) and other subjects throughout this period, and I did too; but Emil was a far more established scholar than I, and he could get away with it in a way that I could not. No matter how radical one's ideas were, no matter how carefully one tried to give off discreet tokens of one's countercultural sympathies, if one were a young and still untenured professor in the sixties, one could not avoid the suspicion that one belonged to "the enemy." After all, one of the catchphrases of the hour was, "Don't trust anyone over thirty!" This was a fight against the status quo, against authority, against "the Establishment"; and, as a youngish, self-declared "radical" clergyman said to me during the period, "You *are* the Establishment!"—though I had barely enough *status* to buy a decent car and went about in ancient vehicles that my students joked about!

The plight of untenured, unpublished, and aspiring university teachers is, I think, one of the untold stories of the sixties. We were a class of neither fish nor fowl. We had to walk a thin line between frankly courting the young and providing our more established colleagues, who would decide our fate, with exaggerated assurances of our solidarity with them and against the rabble-rousers. It was especially difficult for those teaching in the arts and humanities, and in religion or theology the situation was often almost ludicrous. Undergraduates entering courses in physics or geology, unless they were simply ignorant or excessively abrasive, were unlikely to argue with their professors, at least where the subject matter of their disciplines was concerned. But students in the humanities and social sciences were not so constrained by the demands of their disciplines for hard data; and in theology, one soon discovered, every young or not-so-young student claiming personal religious experience was likely, under the influence of the times, to assume a familiarity with the subject matter *at least* as valid as his or her professor's, and likely more authentic on account of its grounding in recent religious experience.

I do not say, as some still do, that the sixties were all bluster and excess. Important changes were made. Unchecked administrative and professorial power, regulations whose legitimacy consisted solely of their longevity, hierarchies of authority that excluded dialogue with those over whom authority was claimed: all that cried out for change. Students did need better representation in matters affecting their own education. "The Establishment," whether in universities, churches, government, or public life generally, did need to be critiqued and, in some instances, openly denounced. *Some* authorities ought to have been called in question long before!

But not all! There were persons of integrity, ability and good will who were unjustly wounded or vilified by these allegedly "liberating" trends and events. I have witnessed good people—*really* good people—reduced to frustration and abject humiliation by the tyranny of the majority. Self-righteous experts in "group dynamics," often persons of mediocre abilities but raised now to prominence by the popularity of groupthink, could reduce strong men and women to tears with a few well-chosen *personal* inquiries. Recognized scholars and gifted administrators could be brought low by being shown to be "out of touch with their feelings," or by having their marital relations exposed. Teachers and church officers whose authority came, not from their office alone, but from internal gifts and hard work, were frequently maligned because they left too little room for "democratic representation," or criticized "evaluations" of their performance that had more to do with popular appeal than with competence. Men and women who were wonderfully qualified for their work, or who had manifested unusual initiative in creating new ventures that benefited others, were often castigated because they refused to turn the administration of their projects over to committees made up of individuals who, while they may indeed have represented this or that marginalized social faction, were clearly incompetent or ill equipped to administer what more creative and experienced minds had begun.

And that brings us again to the so-called SCM Book Room debacle. From the outset it seemed to me and to many other senior friends of the Movement that something must have gone terribly wrong in our beloved SCM when a person of the faith, theological acumen, and personal integrity of Bob Miller could so suddenly become that "terrible man," a "capitalist at heart," who had no sympathy for "democratic traditions," etc., etc. Anyone who reads—attentively—the excerpts from Bob Miller's letters that I have reproduced in this volume—not only the early letters, but the whole lot!—would have to be absurdly biased to believe such accusations. That a man who had devoted years of his life, all the ingenuity he could muster, and unrecorded monetary and other personal resources to the creation of such a valuable service to learning—that such a man might have developed, over the course of the years, a sense of "ownership" should have surprised no one.

The sense of ownership, however, does not always flow from selfish ("capitalist!") motivation; it can flow as well from belief in the larger purpose and worthwhileness of what is being done. It can flow from a profound sense of service—from the *stewardship* of something larger than self and larger than the concerns of the moment.

It is not incidental to this discussion that Bob Miller chose to call himself the book steward. The ancient metaphor of the steward,[1] which is so important for biblical literature (consider its prominence in the parables of Jesus) assumes that the steward, while certainly not in the literal sense owner of that which he is called to care for, must nevertheless bring to that task the kind of personal attention, farsightedness and self-sacrifice that would be displayed by a *truly caring and wise* owner. Stewards, biblically speaking, are not just managers. By biblical standards, today's CEOs, with their ridiculous salaries and outrageous "incentives" are simply "hirelings" (John 10:12): opportunists who have no real loyalty to their corporations but are more than ordinarily driven by personal gain. Real stewards, in biblical parlance, are devoted and faithful representatives of "the householder"—which regularly, in that literature, of course means God. Those who do not understand the logic (or better the *theo*-logic!) of this office would do well to read once more the Joseph narrative of the book of Genesis, followed, perhaps, by Thomas Mann's four-volume novelistic commentary on that most stirring of biblical sagas.[2]

Bob Miller's *stewardship* of the Book Room was the consequence of his devotion to the vision that created the SCM in the first place—which is *not* to be equated with the policies and current interests of this or that board or administration. That vision was centred in the belief that the Christian message demanded

1. See my *The Steward: A Biblical Symbol Come of Age* (1990; reprinted, Eugene, OR: Wipf & Stock, 2004).

2. Or, from more recent usage of the metaphor, when the organizers of the Vancouver Olympics coined the slogan, "own the podium," they obviously did not intend this in a literal sense but rather that our Canadian athletes should be so serious and dedicated in their various competitions that their wins might inspire our much-beleaguered country to new levels of belief in itself. "Ownership" in this sense is not an end in itself but a means to a greater goal.

of all who took it seriously a devotion to *study*: the study of the Scriptures, the study of the history and theological traditions of the church, and the study of the literature, arts and culture of the socio-historical context—the *here and now* in which this message seeks a hearing. The vision that gave rise to the SCM combined the inherent demands of faith for *understanding* with an equal recognition of the fact that study, the dedicated human quest for knowledge and wisdom, was of the essence of the university. The fact that the SCM of Canada had at the national level a permanent secretariat for *study* was a direct consequence of this vision. It was the belief of the Movement's founders and international supporters that a Christian presence in the universities of the world should be entirely compatible with *the purpose of the university as such*. It should not seek to impose on universities some system of belief or method of inquiry incongruous with the university's own ideals; rather, it should attempt to serve and enhance the university's own aim to investigate all sources of and claims to knowledge, and to issue in the preparation of the young for mature contributions to society as a whole. Questions of Christian faith and its ethical consequences were not only the prerogative of believers but belonged to all who have membership in a civilization whose history, culture and institutions are steeped, for both good and ill, in various interpretations and expressions of this faith. The very idea of the university has its origins in the belief of the Judeo-Christian tradition that human beings are called to, and capable of, understanding; and specifically in the medieval scholastic insistence that *truth is one* (hence, *uni*versity). Neither Christianity nor any other religion has the right to a place on the university campus if its purpose is to proselytize or evangelize or exercise extraneous power of any kind, and the SCM at its best has never sought such goals. But since its overarching mission is only to enhance the university's own stated aim, that is, to pursue truth and understanding—in short, to *study!*—the SCM is not an intruder in the halls of Academe but a voluntary community of service to its host. Christian faith insists that understanding, when it is serious, must manifest itself in action: theology without ethics is false theology; faith without works is dead (James 2:17). But this does not translate immediately into this or that specific program of political action that all Christians are required to adopt forthwith and by which their faith itself is judged. The reduction of Christian faith to morality, whether personal or socio-political morality, has occurred all too often in Christian history, and it was part of what was happening to the Canadian SCM in the sixties. Study—a quest for understanding that did justice to both the faith and the university—was being replaced by an activism that frequently *spurned* study as passivity and a mere avoidance of action. The breadth of inquiry and curiosity about the world that was represented in the book store built up, over the years, by Bob Miller, was in danger of being exchanged for narrowly conceived and ideologically-inspired literature attuned to the dominant values and concerns of the most vociferous.

It is simplistic to lay the blame for the Book Store crisis at the door of the students, including the student leadership of the period, but more particularly the bulk of the student membership of the SCM, which had very little notion of what was transpiring. Though it is to be hoped that the young, as they mature, will raise critical questions about their own youthful enthusiasms, it seems to me clear that at the time of the crisis the students—collectively—were playing the roles that the *Zeitgeist* was writing for them, even (and perhaps especially) when they thought they were being extraordinarily original. The student world is notoriously impermanent and fluid. Today's students have little or no knowledge of what happened in their lecture halls, playing fields, student councils and residences even a decade earlier—to say nothing of the origins and traditions of a movement like the SCM.

More questionable are the parts played by adults who gained some kind of satisfaction as witnesses and cheerleaders of these eventualities. At least a few of these adults had nursed old resentments and grudges which now, in the context of public controversy and accusation, they could openly or covertly enact. Like every charismatic person, Bob Miller had attracted many who were at the same time dependent upon his friendship and approval and resentful of their dependency. And there were others who, having risen to new levels of prominence on account of the very vacuum of authority that was a consequence of this 'rebellion,' were glad to play the role of seeming peacemakers and reconcilers, though it entailed leaving the primary victim of the fracas bereft of many on whom he felt he could count for sympathy and support. It is of course an old, old story, and one that readers of the New Testament ought to understand very well indeed!

Bob Miller was a sophisticated thinker who knew that old story intimately. But I believe that he was nevertheless rather taken by surprise at the turn of events, the rapidity with which it developed into a crisis, and the intensity of the passions that were displayed.[3] For years as study secretary he had been received with enthusiasm and affection by student groups on every campus in the country; and now, particularly at the vaunted 'show-down' in Edmonton (National Council, May 1975), he was treated not only as an "enemy of the people" but practically a lawbreaker! Bob was better able than most to camouflage his deepest personal feelings in critical moments, but I know that this almost total reversal of the trust and gratitude he had experienced in his work with the Student Christian Movement hurt him deeply and left a permanent scar upon his life. If the word *tragic* is at all applicable to this whole sorry affair, the genesis of which lies in the chaos of the times and in the *pathetic* incapacity of good and intelligent people to discern truth through the dust of battle—if, I say, the word *tragic*

3. I quoted Paul Warner earlier as saying that the situation actually "frightened" Bob—a man, as all who knew him would attest, was not given to "fright"! But it *is* frightening to think that one could be taken to court and vilified by self-important "witnesses," some of them alleged friends, who might well be able to garner the "spirit of the times" to achieve exceptional sympathy for their "cause."

One such ready witness, a person both well known and highly respected in church circles, telephoned the SCM offices to ask what she ought to do if and when the SCM took Miller and his associates to court. When she was reminded by a colleague sympathetic to Bob that what she really ought to do, as one who had *actually been present* at the time of the informal agreement that established the complete independence of the SCM Book Room, would be straightway to testify to that fact! The "old friend of the Movement" hung up.

can be used at all in this connection, it should be used only to describe the sense of collapse and disillusionment that Bob Miller was caused to endure. Fortunately, he was humanly and as a person of faith able to move beyond tragedy. The real pathos of this drama, however, is what these powerful currents of the age did to the Movement that had been such a bright star in the educational experiences of so many.

2

The second way in which the life of Robert Miller—or more accurately the public *image* of that life—has been detrimentally affected by the character of the age in which it was lived has to do with a subject that I would prefer not to discuss; it is necessary to discuss it despite my misgivings, however, because it lingers in the consciousness and (to speak plainly) the *gossip* of many, and as such carriers with it far too much weight. I refer to speculation concerning the so-called sexual identity of Bob Miller. For some it is a "given" that Bob Miller was "gay." Some claim to know a good deal about the matter—for instance that Bob "discovered" his homosexual orientation rather late in time, that he was disturbed by the discovery and tried to alter his "orientation," etc., etc. One or two announce that Bob divulged his homosexual orientation publicly, or at least rather openly; and at least one person attributes this reputed "coming out" to his own influence upon Bob—in his view, of course, a salutary influence, a sort of victory for truth! On the other hand, some of Bob's oldest and closest friends are sceptical of the certainty with which such views are held, and others express genuine puzzlement: "Where did this opinion that Bob was homosexual come from?" asks one man who knew Bob longer than almost anyone.

In what follows, I do not intend to answer the question, was Bob Miller gay? For one thing, I would not know what to answer such a question—I never discussed the matter with Bob himself; for another, as I shall try to explain, I regard the question itself as "loaded," misleading, and highly problematic. I belong to that generation of Canadian farm and working people whose curiosity about the sexual habits of others was still held in check by a certain respect for human dignity and privacy. In short, we felt it was "none of our business" to snoop about in the bedrooms of our friends.

What *does* interest me, however, is why this question and its resolution has such a hold—I would even say a *morbid* hold—on people in our time. Why, as it applies not only to Bob Miller but to nearly everyone else, has sexuality achieved such prominence in our culture, and, more particularly, how does this inordinate preoccupation with sex affect the way we think about others—and about ourselves?

One does not have to agree with the entire philosophy of Michel Foucault to find intriguing and suggestive his statement that "'Sexuality' is an invention of the modern state, the industrial revolution, and capitalism." Sexuality should not be analyzed only in biological or psychological terms, Foucault believed; the most important perspective on the subject can be gained only through the study of *history*. From a broad historical vantage point, which takes into account not only previous ages in the evolution of "the West" but also other civilizations and peoples, it is necessary to conclude that "this thing we now call sexuality came into existence in the eighteenth-century West and did not exist previously in this form."[4]

This seems to me a viable thesis. What interests me, however, is not only the fact that sexuality is a historical category, thoroughly conditioned the dominant pursuits and values of our social context, but why it is that, especially though not exclusively in North America, we have allowed sexuality to become the *defining component* of the human being. In doing so, we have effectively jettisoned both of the founding cultural traditions of our civilization—the tradition of Athens, which despite variations would hold to Aristotle's view that "*Man* (the human being) is a <u>rational</u> *animal*"; and the tradition of Jerusalem, which regards the human person as *imago Dei*, that is, as a creature capable of unique relationship with

4. See Foucault's *History of Sexuality.*

its Creator and other creatures). For a society to devote the kind of attention and valuation to sex that ours has, surely these ancient conceptions of essential humanity, though rhetorically still honoured as foundational assumptions, must have been quietly shunted aside or discarded altogether. If our very *identity* is determined primarily by the character of our sexual fantasies and behaviour, then what significance does "rationality" or "relationality" have for us? What does it matter that we are "speaking" animals (*homo loquens*) or "playing" animals (*homo ludens*)—or even, for that matter, that we have opposable thumbs and cook our food?

It may be argued that the premise of this statement is exaggerated—that as a culture we are not *that* fixated on sex or willing to define others, or have ourselves defined, by the myriad of categories relating to sex: sex appeal, sexual orientation, the sexual "spectrum," sexual activity, the frequency of sexual gratification, and so on. One may agree that *individuals* can and do, in some cases, resist this narrow categorization, and that to a greater or lesser extent thinking persons are usually able to maintain a certain critical vigilance about the power of sexual considerations in every field of human endeavour—politics, religion, law, education, the arts, communications, and the like. But throughout the twentieth century, in a way that was not true the nineteenth or even of my youth, we have been deluged with sexual manifestations and images of every sort. No film can afford to leave it out, and every advertisement that hopes to engage the public must employ sexual imagery in blatant or subtle form. An orgy of post-Freudian analysis of every conceivable type of sexual behaviour has spawned whole university departments. The passion for classification and nomenclature that Linnaeus in the eighteenth century brought to botany and Darwin in the nineteenth brought to the origin and evolution of species, thousands of social scientists, psychiatrists, and "sexologists" have in the twentieth century and beyond brought to the naming of every actual or conceivable form of sexuality. And while neither Carl Linnaeus nor Charles Darwin was ready to expand his scientific findings into a whole worldview, the modern explorers of human sexuality seem to have achieved a remarkably comprehensive finality about humankind: We are *sexual* animals, we are told—which, since all animal life involves sexuality, must be judged a tautology. I do not suggest that this triumph of the sexual component has been the direct result of scientific investigation or even pseudoscientific speculation. Many of the individual thinkers who have helped to explore this previously hidden continent of sex, including Freud, have been aware of other aspects of the human psyche and human behaviour; but once again the spirit of the age has shown such a predisposition—such a prurient interest, one could say—in everything sexual that the West has paid far more attention to Freud and other explorers of the dark continent of sensuality than to Darwin or Einstein or the exploration of outer space. If not "the West" as a whole, at least very large segments of the population of the modern Western world are prone to consider sexuality the most decisive aspect of the life of our species and of individual life.[5]

The extent and effect of this elevation of sexuality to a place of primacy in the popular mind are most conspicuous and poignant where homosexuality is concerned. Like many other humanly approachable teachers, clergy, or counselors, I have quite often been made the recipient of sexual confidences on the part of some of my students and other acquaintances. In the 1950s and into the next decade, those sharing such confidences were usually hesitant and wary. But with the growing openness about all things sexual, these "confessions" became increasingly straightforward or even bold.

5. It could be asked, for instance, why it is that the present sex scandals in the Roman Catholic Church have achieved the public attention that they have. I realize that this subject entails a host of considerations beyond sexuality as such—especially the whole matter of hierarchic authority and an ecclesiology that puts the "protection" of the church (Christ's body, after all!) above the protection of children. Yet it cannot be overlooked that the public in both North America and Europe is far more fascinated (*fixated* would not be out of place in this connection!) by any hint of sexual misconduct on the part of priests than by any other subject involving the life of the church in the modern world. Observing the way in which the media pounce upon every shred of news about the priestly abuse of minors, one could conclude that the entire priesthood is awash in sexual aberration and that the church as a whole performs no trustworthy or noble human service.

Sometimes one had the impression that the act of divulging this intimate glimpse into another life had about it a disturbing if slight hint of flattery, and perhaps of superiority. "I have been sharing with some of my good friends—and I wanted to share with you, professor—the fact that I am . . . gay." The hint of superiority usually lay, I think, with the sense of moral victory ("honesty") felt by the subject, though on occasion it extended to the suggestion that "gay" might even constitute a higher form of life, since so many of the great artists, musicians, writers, and public figures were now known to have been such.

I don't think that I *ever* displayed a judgemental or a shocked countenance in the presence of such confidences, though I was on occasion surprised. The sexual lives of most people are at least complex, if they are not full of pathos. Where sex is concerned, Reinhold Niebuhr used to tell his classes, using the words of Scripture, "there is none righteous, no not one" (Romans 3:10).

Yet one was nearly always saddened, and sometimes deeply saddened, by such confessions. Because what one was being told was not only that one's student or friend had engaged in such and such homosexual acts, but that this (usually relatively young) person believed that he or she *was* "a homosexual." Given the social context, such a confession bore the weight of ultimacy, finality, personal and ontological closure!

"Why," I often asked, "when you *are so many things,* have you chosen this one aspect of your being to *define* your being? The verb 'to be' is the trickiest, often the most deceptive, yet in the last analysis the weightiest of all verbs. To be sure, in ordinary discourse we use it frequently and without a thought—'I am cold,' 'I am bored,' 'She is kind hearted,' 'He is cute,' etc. But you have come here with a message that does not fall into the category of casual discourse. You are in full ontological mode! 'I *am* gay. Gay is who and what I *am.* Full stop.

"Presumably," I sometimes continued, "you are also somebody's child, somebody's friend, somebody's student—maybe you are even a good student! You are (for example) Caucasian, a citizen of Canada, a child of the twenty-first century. Are you not also a

Christian?—a Jew?—an atheist? Did I not hear that you are a good writer?—a musician?—a student of history? I understand you write poems. You *are* in fact a great many things, qualities, experiences, beliefs, fears, hopes, ambitions, relationships . . . etc. Why, out of all the things you are, have you chosen to define yourself so explicitly and so narrowly in these sexual terms?"

It is a rhetorical question. I know why this has happened. It has happened because this has become the definitive quality and attribute of our Western technocracy. It has happened because others "out there" (your friends, your contemporaries, the girls, the boys, the gay lobby, your church, perhaps even your own parents) have been waiting for you to "declare" yourself, to move to one side or the other of this great cultural/psychological divide. It has happened because it is comforting *for you,* given the spirit of the age, to resolve that certain niggling ambiguity you have experienced within yourself (Where on "the spectrum" am I?). Now you have crossed that threshold, made that decision, stepped into that other country: half the world—the world of the opposite sex—is no longer a challenge, no longer a threat, to you. You are gay. Period. Persons of the opposite sex need not apply! Case closed.

But one is sad, in such situations, not only because one is witnessing someone's readiness to exchange *the essential mystery* of his or her person for an unworthy mess of pottage whose chief ingredient is a simplistic understanding of sexuality;[6] more significantly one is saddened by the fact that, as a society, we have allowed sexuality—that is, specific sexual fantasies, acts, and

6. Alfred Kinsey may be faulted on several counts (e.g., that he limited his testing too narrowly to certain classes), but I have the impression that his general belief about the falsity of assuming absolute distinctions between "heterosexual" and "homosexual" persons has been vindicated by most later studies. "Males do not represent two discrete populations, heterosexual and homosexual. The world is not to be divided into sheep and goats. Not all things are black nor all things white. Only the human mind invents categories and tries to force facts into separated pigeonholes. The living world is a continuum in each and every one of its aspects. The sooner we learn this concerning human sexual behavior the sooner we shall reach a sound understanding of the realities of sex" (*Sexual Behavior in the Human Male* [Philadelphia: Saunders 1948], 639.)

lifestyles—to become the defining value of our humanity. We have created a society in which persons are identified by their sexual thoughts, words, deeds, and "body language." A name is mentioned at a dinner party and a chorus of voices announce, "Oh yes, he's gay," or "Isn't she a lesbian?" Students go to hear a professor of literature, not because of his expertise on Milton, but out of curiosity about his "gayness." How would a "gay" teach Shakespeare? The liberally minded cultivate a number of gay or lesbian friends—it's cool! Recently I heard of a fourteen-year-old girl who was being considered for an important television drama. "Do you have any *gay* friends?" asked the "hip" interviewer. In this case, however, the little girl had somehow acquired a wisdom beyond her years. "Well, I have *friends*." She answered. (There may be hope for the generations still to come!)

Meanwhile, the high suicide rate among youth in Canada, the United States, and other Western countries includes large numbers of young men, especially, who are so persuaded of their problematic sexuality that they cannot face life with courage.

I am among those who celebrate the fact that people today can express their homosexuality openly, without fear of imprisonment or scandal or even, in most cases, grave public scorn. I am an enthusiastic supporter of my denomination's decision that homosexual orientation should not, as such, be a barrier to ordination. I am very glad that our society has achieved a great deal more maturity and compassion about all this than was the case in my childhood and youth, when homosexuality was still "the love that dared not speak its name." I support the right of homosexually inclined persons to marry.

But did the price for this new openness and acceptance of difference have to be the raising up of sexuality to the axiological heights of human striving and desire? Was it necessary, in acquiring a greater maturity about the variety of sexual behaviour, to elevate this particular component of our humanity to such an exalted status? Poor little sex was never intended for divinity! Surely one of the primary objects of serious Christian ethics today should be the *dethronement of sex!* In the realm of personal ethics, at least, no more *political* goal can be imagined; for its implementation would certainly involve a monumental struggle against the "capitalist" (Foucault) forces that deploy and degrade sex for purposes of economic gain, including the huge "entertainment" industry.

This is a struggle that Christians can join without courting either prudery or joylessness. For Christians affirm that the *essence* of human being resides in the mystery of a complex selfhood that cannot be reduced to any or all of its components. Jean-Paul Sartre was simply wrong! Existence does *not* precede essence. We are *not* just our deeds! And we are certainly not just our *sexual* deeds!

Was Bob Miller gay? It is, I must conclude, *the question itself* that is the problem! Preoccupation with that question, wherever and however and about whomsoever it is asked, is demeaning of human intelligence, because it obscures and limits all the other aspects of human existence that ought to take precedence over sexuality. In fact it entails an almost demonic reductionism that is an affront to all the high anthropologies and expectations that have ever been enucleated in the stormy history of our strange and maybe impossible species—anthropologies and expectations that were born out of the hope and the determination that human being might yet attain the glory—"a little lower than the angels"— for which its Creator made it: that it might become truly *rational, wise* (*homo sapiens!*), spontaneously playful (*homo ludens!*), rich in words and speech (*homo loquens!*), and above all abundant in loving relationships (*imago Dei!*) With our cheap and puerile and "culturally-generated" enthroning of an historically-conditioned conceptualization of sexuality, we have belittled ourselves, sold our human birthright for a mess of psychobabble, and soiled even our sexuality.

Was Bob Miller gay? I do not know, and at a profound level I do not care! For *if* the term *homosexual* (that adjective-become-noun!) has any application whatsoever to him, I know with certainty that Bob Miller was *much more than that*! His sexuality, *whatever it was*, doesn't even touch the essence of the one who was, for me and for countless others, a messenger. And it certainly doesn't affect the message he carried and embodied, the message namely of freedom from fates and demons and addictions of every ilk, and of freedom *for* love of God, life, and one another.

3

Who then *was* Bob Miller? How should one honour his memory? What words can be found—words that, while they certainly cannot capture his essence, can point in the right direction, can be thought symbolically true, or can at least help to guard against false images and misrepresentations of this profoundly human person?

It is well known among his friends, as we've seen, that Bob admired the works of Albert Camus. Not that he would ever claim expertise where that author was concerned. "Next week I have to give a lecture on Camus," he wrote to me in October 1959, and added "—which ought to be a laugh, if not an embarrassment to all concerned." Yet he was drawn to this author, I think, as he had been drawn to few others—excepting perhaps Barth. One had the impression that he felt Camus spoke to him, and perhaps even *for* him.

There is of course a good deal of discussion among the pundits about Camus himself—who *he* was, where he belonged in the scheme of things. Many claimed him for "existentialism," but the guru of that philosophic/literary genre, Jean-Paul Sartre, denied Camus entrance to that high temple: Camus, Sartre pronounced, was a classical pessimist. But so was Augustine—so far as human possibilities are concerned; so to say that Camus was an atheist, as some do, does not follow necessarily from his pessimistic anthropology. We could spend a good deal of time trying to define *pessimism*, but it would be better, I think, simply to recognize that Camus was and remains a rather unique thinker who defies categorization. As does Bob Miller.

On one of our last visits with him in Victoria, as I have mentioned earlier, Bob was particularly animated about Camus's *The First Man*, a previously unpublished work that the son and daughter of the author had withheld from the public for thirty-five years for broadly political reasons. The manuscript was in his car with Camus when he was killed. *The First Man* is Camus's own recollections of his childhood and adolescence, and what especially fascinated Bob Miller was the author's testimony to the singular influence upon him of one of his teachers, a man without whose teaching and encouragement the world would have had no "Camus."

Fortunately, the editors of the book, Camus's children, have seen fit to include, in its final pages, two letters. One, dated 19 November 1957, is from Camus himself. He had just been awarded the Nobel Prize in Literature and, after allowing "the commotion around [him] to subside a bit," he wanted to write to his dear teacher, Monsieur [Louis] Germain: "Without you," he wrote, "without the affectionate hand you extended to the small poor child that I was, without your teaching, and your example, none of all this would have happened."

It will be understood by the reader by this time, I think, that when I first read it I was able to identify with that confession in a quite personal way. But what interests me more just at this point is the response of the teacher. M. Germain had just received yet another book about his famous pupil. "I have not yet read this work, other than the first few pages," he wrote, but it was enough to evoke his reflection on the subject of this growing Camus industry: "Who is Camus? I have the impression that those who try to penetrate your nature do not quite succeed. You have always shown an instinctive reticence about revealing your nature, your feelings. You succeed all the more for being unaffected, direct."

These words could have been written about Bob Miller—*and also about the various attempts to 'penetrate <u>his</u> nature,' including, certainly, this one!* Bob's "instinctive reticence about revealing [his] nature, [his] feelings" could be overlooked only by the most insensitive. It was just this reticence, I think, that simultaneously intrigued and frustrated those around him. For reasons of our own—a variety of reasons—we, most of us, wanted to know more about the inner Miller self, the self beyond the brown, sagacious eyes. We knew that "feelings" were there—likely very deep ones. But for the most part we had to be satisfied with signs and sighs and facial expressions and raised shoulders and a few barely audible words. And that wretched "unaffected *directness*"!

Once, I remember, I tried to force him into revealing, a little, the subjectivity, the inwardness, that I knew was there. The circumstances were such that, for me at least, it was natural—even necessary!—to find out whether my own sense of 'unknowing' had any echo in him, this one who had already taught me much. We were sitting in a car just outside my parents' home in Woodstock. My father had died two weeks earlier, and we had just come from yet another funeral, that of a good friend. I felt bereft of understanding, empty, on the verge of cynicism. The *absence*—the so *sudden* absence!—of my father only accentuated the question his *presence* had always posed. Could one know anyone else, really? Who was my father, *really? And who was I for my father?* Why could I never break through the formalities and set patterns of our relationship and feel, at last, that I had encountered the *person* my father was? And now he *was* no more. The possibility of meeting him *person to person* no longer existed. I would never know, really, who my father had been, or what I had signified for him. I was left with nothing more substantial than a huge bundle of incongruous memories—memories mainly of conflict, tension, and repressed anger made all the more eloquent on account of my father's periodic signs of approval, pride, and even love.

I knew that Bob Miller understood all this—and at more than a superficial level. After all, his own father had left the family while young, too. But I felt the need for *words*! "How does one *know* anyone else?" I demanded. "What about *you*?—do you know, for instance, your brother Doug?" Silence. Then, "Well, I know a lot *about* him," Bob answered. But that is all he said.

I had realized before that Bob did not (could not?) appreciate too much introspection, subjectivity. The reader may remember that in one of his earliest letters he warned me very gently but plainly against too much "inwardness": "One thing to be said is that you will always be somewhat too introspective and full of fears and doubts and questionings about what you do or say. Just because this has its value, it becomes a temptation to some of us. I would say to you now, the more that you can get away from such introspection and questioning, and get on with the job at hand, the better. The more we can substitute the searching of the Bible for the searching of our own philosophy, the better."[7]

Sixty years after I first read these words, I can admit—and gladly—not only their truth but their pastoral sensitivity. Introspection, soul-searching, perpetual questioning, doubt—this has indeed been my "temptation"; it is still my temptation, though I have learned, fortunately, to be less taken off guard by the "thoughts that wound from behind" (Kierkegaard). And yet . . .?

And yet I wonder now (I could not have done so in 1949!) whether I'd have become what I became—a Christian theologian—had it not been for this temptation. I am comforted by the phrase by which Bob Miller seems to acknowledge that he too was somewhat familiar with this temptation—that it is "a temptation to *some of us.*" But I also realize now (I could not have done so in 1949) that the antidote Bob suggests for combating this temptation, while in a certain sense—yes, an authentically *Christian* sense—right and true, is one that I could never have emulated with anything like consistency. In this particular excerpt he identifies that antidote a stricter attention to the Bible; elsewhere he stresses what is only hinted at here in the phrase "get on with the job at hand," namely absorption in work, the care of others—obedience!

The word *obedience* is one of the great, central, almost sacred words of Calvinism; and it is not accidental that Bob had recourse to it several times in his early letters to me; for, at least in this phase of his pilgrimage, he was thinking very much in the Calvinistic mode. His special mentor, as we've noted, was Karl Barth—perhaps made present and forceful in a certain way by Ellen Flesseman. Barth was not a Calvinist, exclusively, in his early writings, but one can easily notice a process of what I call Calvinization as his work progresses. In at least one place he vehemently eschews the "existentialist screaming" (Kierkegaard included) that had influenced his early work too much. "Calvinization" is even more

---

7. Written from the Alumneum at Hebelstr. 17, Basel, Switzerland on October 27, 1949.

visible in the reception of his thought by his avowedly closest fol-
lowers, the "Barthians." I would never say that Bob Miller was in
that overzealous sense a Barthian; he was too conscious of the variety of Christian and human witness for that—a consciousness that
shows itself later in the motto he chose for his book store, 'Beware
the man of one book.'[8] Bob admired Calvin not only as the most
consistent and rigorous *thinker* of the Reformation, but as one who
translated his theology into a program of action. "At least," he said
to me once when I was being a little snide about Calvin, "Calvin
tried to do something about Geneva!" He didn't mean the Geneva
of today, which is almost appallingly decent and well ordered, but
the tumultuous crossroads of conflicting forces that Geneva certainly was in the sixteenth century when Guillaume Farel urged
the young author of *The Institutes of the Christian Religion*, who
was passing through, to stay there and put things to rights.

It is probable that Bob and I, had we had the good fortune to
live in closer proximity to each other throughout our lives, would
have found ourselves on different "wavelengths" fairly often; for
unlike him I was driven to investigate the interiority of the self
rather consistently, and indeed I could not imagine a *theology* that
avoids "introspection." In this I followed not Calvin but Luther,
who said that he had become a theologian by going where his
temptations took him. Though I admired Barth, and was once even
considered "the Barthian" (the only one in captivity!) at Union
Seminary, I found, as I aged, that the great Swiss theologian had
become so very "Christian" that he seemed no longer to remember
the confused mass of ambiguity, longing, and despair in which ordinary human life is steeped. "I wish," he once said, "that someone
would whisper to Paul Tillich that he ought not to take his doubts
so seriously." But Tillich, the teacher with whom I struggled most
and therefore, in the long run, learned most from, understood the
conflicting "polarities" (his word) that beset our creaturely existence—love and hate, faith and doubt, hope and despair, reason
and sensuality, the will and the courage to live and the *Todestrieb*
(death wish) and all the rest; and therefore he was able to speak to

8. *Homo unius libri timeo*, an expression attributed to St Thomas Aquinas.

post-Christendom, secular people in a way that Karl Barth could not. It was not incidental that Bob Miller was gently critical of me when I wrote from Saskatoon that I was finding Tillich increasingly important as I tried to *teach* theology. Bob responded (as the reader may recall) with typical Milleresque humor-*cum*-innuendo, that it seemed the flat prairie landscape was exercising an inordinate influence on my theology, since the Barthian heights and the Tillichian valleys were now, apparently, leveling off into a plain! Oddly, he never talked about Tillich in my presence, though Tillich had been one of his teachers too.

Probably we are touching here on an important distinction in types of human character and behaviour, though most of the terms that are used for this (*introvert/extrovert, interiority/exteriority, contemplative/activist*, etc.) are quite unsatisfactory; I think, however, that it helps to understand Bob Miller a little better if one realizes that he did not feel comfortable in the presence of too much "introspection," too immodest a display of "feelings," too much "personal confession." I sat with him and another friend for at least two hours, one evening long ago, while the friend poured out her heart to him, and later he told me, "I didn't know half the time what she was talking about." To be honest, I didn't either; but at that stage in our relationship I was only an uninformed young bystander in such encounters between old acquaintances. On another occasion, I myself tried late one night as we sat in the manse in a small Ontario town where I was student assistant, to tell Bob about the awkward and complicated relationship into which, quite unintentionally, I had fallen vis a vis a young widow whose loneliness had led her to entertain certain ideas about me. For me, it was a real dilemma. But while Bob listened with (I thought) interest, he had nothing to say to me, no help to offer. A similar situation was experienced by our mutual friend, George Grant, who, when he discovered the trick that had been played on him when he left his philosophy chair at Dalhousie for one at York University (*viz.*, that he was expected to use as his text for a major course a book he despised, written by the department head!) sought out Bob Miller in the hope of finding a sympathetic ear. After half an hour of trying to share his chagrin, disappointment, and anger with Bob, George realized that he would receive no counsel from this source, and perhaps not even very much sympathy. Like Nicodemus, the great Canadian philosopher "went away sorrowful."

Yet having exemplified in this way "the quiet Kierkegaardian," I am immediately conscious of the one-sidedness of the statement these examples might attribute to our subject. As Bob's early letters to me in particular show, his capacity to put himself into the shoes of another (in this case, the village boy making his way in a large city, and trying to make hard vocational choices) was quite extraordinary. It is probable, however, that his capacity for empathy was more natural in some situations than in others—which would certainly not be unusual. For one thing, I believe that Bob was more comfortable with ordinary people than with more complex individuals—academics and the like! He once confided to me that when he was alone with Emil Fackenheim he never knew what to talk about. With Rose Fackenheim, on the other hand, he was entirely at home—and I think he was often more at home with women than with men, especially women like Rose, Ellen Flesseman, and others who were highly articulate and who, because they simply enjoyed being with him, did not depend overmuch on Bob's verbal responses to the thoughts they voiced. With such persons as, in another way, with the WoodGreen young people and the modest undergrads at Western and my own brothers and mother, I always sensed that Bob Miller was entirely comfortable. But I think he did not respond so freely and positively to situations in which he sensed certain expectations of greater self-giving, verbal intimacy, or spiritual affinity on his part.

This, insofar as it is true, ought not necessarily to suggest limitation, even though it might have been felt to be such by those involved. Not everyone is cut out for the role of confessor or confidante, and certainly not in all circumstances. I believe Bob knew that about himself. Far too many people clamored for his sympathies, and he was realistic enough to know that he could not help most of them. Again from my own history of our friendship I can cite an instance of his reluctance to pretend greater abilities than he knew he possessed. In my thirtieth year, after months of intense study in preparation for my doctoral comprehensive examinations, I suffered a nervous collapse that quite unnerved me (it is often associated with year thirty!). It was a new experience for me, and in its immediate aftermath, while I was visiting in Toronto briefly, I told Bob about it—or tried to. But I hadn't got far when he retorted, "Well, if you feel anxious about it, you'd better talk to a psychiatrist." I know that he did not intend this as a rebuff or put-down; he just knew that he was not able to deal with that sort of thing—and that is a knowledge that many would-be counselors, perhaps especially among the clergy, do not possess.

And finally in trying to understand the "silent" Bob Miller, one should recognize, I think, that Bob was one of those persons who had a certain appreciation of and need for solitude. One often sensed this in his presence, and I suspect that it could be seen already in the child that he once was. In one of his letters from Victoria to Mary McInroy, he wrote: "I really feel like being away off on an island apart from the world. I guess I have always been somewhat apart from it anyway."[9] That the sense of apartness increased as he aged seems to me not only understandable but almost inevitable. I am old enough myself now to realize that solitude is necessary to whatever one can acquire by way of tranquility of spirit—especially if one is given to reflection, and especially in this very noisy and restless age in which we live! I can well imagine that the hours Bob Miller spent contemplating his "orientalia" (Paul Warner said that he regularly rose at four a.m. and studied his scrolls and pictures for several hours) were full of meaning and contentment for him. He would have distinguished this contemplation quite sharply, I think, from "introspection"; in fact oriental art in particular rather discourages precisely any kind of morbid subjectism.

But I imagine that this preference for solitude was present in him long before he became an old man. Evelyn Reid recounts, in this connection, a very illuminating episode:

9. Letter is dated simply "Mon. evening."

One incident with Bob that had a strong influence on me follows: he was telling me about some place, some thing. I shared my interest and said that I would like to do that WITH someone. He could not understand that necessity, he disagreed. He wanted to know, why not alone? Anyway, this brought to mind the many times Bob did things noticeably alone—not lonely, but alone. How many people do you know who go to the opera alone, to New York alone, to five operas in one week or two, and not talk about it? He didn't resist company but he had a stronger capacity for aloneness than most people. This has always been observable, but often mis-read. Detached? [No], He was comfortable with himself. That is a trait that many people cannot accept.[10]

I find Evelyn's observation both a keen and a credible one. As I told her, however, I would like to add one caveat: I doubt that Bob was as *consistently* "comfortable with himself" as Evelyn's generalization might suggest. I do think that he usually enjoyed his solitude, and sought to protect himself from the gregarious and the demanding. But I heard in many of his words and "sighs too deep for words" a certain longing—*Sehnsucht* is the German word for what I mean. I think, for instance, he envied some of us who are married and have children. I know that he was very grateful for the long "fraternal relationship"[11] that he had with Paul Warner. Paul's practical know-how as well as his personal compatibility and care ensured that Bob would have a comfortable and relatively worry-free retirement. Bob was not one to live in the world that "might have been," and he never said anything to me or in my hearing that would suggest melancholy disappointment with his lot; yet particularly when he made allusion, as he did fairly often, to our children and the family life that Rhoda and I were given, I felt the presence in him of a kind of yearning, or perhaps just the memory of a yearning, that had never quite vanished. Perhaps that early love affair that was not allowed to continue and blossom was indeed (as

10. Email to me dated March 17, 2010.

11. Mary McInroy's term (her letter to me of March-April 2010).

Paul Warner expressed it) a more "tragic" reality in Bob's personal history than most of us knew.

4

As I consider how best I might bring this attempt at remembrance to a close, I cannot suppress a feeling of embarrassment—almost of guilt—that I have dared to write so much about a friend who, among my many acquaintances, I would have to consider in many ways the most elusive. To admit that my account is biased, even prejudiced, and certainly very much *my* account, is so axiomatic that it is hardly worth saying. Others will have their memories, and some will be quite different from mine. But *all* will fall far short of the object, who was, after all, a living subject, a 'thou' and no 'thing'—to use Buber's language. We must all resort to personal experience when we try to describe another human being, and that means that we shall accentuate that, in our account of the other, which was most significant for us, each one, personally. For me, as I've stated from the outset, Bob Miller was the bearer of a message—by which I do not mean a single, simple bit of news, easily codified and delivered once only. For at the deepest level I am speaking about the kerygma, the "good news," the gospel, the *Christian* message; and that message, while it may be heard in a dramatic or decisive way on some one, initial, perhaps even datable, occasion, for the most part has to be heard many times and in many different circumstances and therefore in a great variety of words and deeds—and in symbols and presences and intimations, in sights (art) and sounds (music) that are beyond the power of words (but let us not denigrate words, either!)

Bob Miller alerted me to a whole "strange new world" (Barth) from our first meeting on that island of the beautiful sun; but had he not followed that initial hearing with those thoughtful letters from Europe, and then fifty-five years' worth of friendship and fraternal watchfulness *over every significant turn of my life*, it is quite possible that the first hearing of what I sensed might be a special, destiny-laden "message" for me would soon have faded and been forgotten. Had not the messenger been as well the *mentor,* the message might never have taken!

Nor was Bob Miller the only messenger who carried this great and scarcely credible message my way. The sermons of Arthur Young—beautiful, literate, profound sermons—watered the seed that Bob planted (1 Corinthians 3:6). The person and concrete street-witness of the ministry of Ray McCleary gave moral specificity and ethical clarity to the message. The unforgettable teachers who taught me over a long apprenticeship of eleven years of study, particularly Bennett and Scherer and Tillich and Niebuhr and Pauck and Terrien and Muilenburg and the other great scholars at Union Seminary in New York during the 1950s; the people of my one and only parish who were "just people, but that's something"; some of the students during forty years of college, seminary, and university teaching; countless persons I met along the way, both famous and unknown persons; and more than any others a certain lady who was at one time a close colleague of SCM study secretary, Robert Miller—well, one as slow-witted and heart-stubborn and prone-to-melancholy as I required and still requires *countless* messengers if anything like "Good News" is to be heard!

Yet it remains that the first of these messengers has a special place in one's memory, if only as an elusive presence *about* whom one may know a good deal without being able comfortably and confidently to announce (as people often do) 'Oh yes, I knew him! I knew him very well!'

Dietrich Bonhoeffer, thirteen years Bob Miller's senior— a man whom neither Bob nor I ever met but whose words have touched both of us, and many others, profoundly—offers the only answer, I think, that can rightly apply to our knowledge of others— *and of ourselves.* The only acceptable *Christian* answer, I mean.

Bonhoeffer wrote a wonderful poem in his prison cell while he awaited death at the hands of the Nazis just days before the allied victory. It is probably not to be judged "great poetry," but the theological wisdom and human depth of the poem trump all claims to greatness in poetry. The poem is titled "Wer bin ich?"— "Who Am I?" Thrown in upon himself, cut off from others, the young man (he was just thirty-nine) faces the question that we all face—or fail to face, refuse, perhaps, to face: the question of his own identity. The Christ faced it too, and he made his disciples face it—"Who do people say that I am?" "Who do *you* say that I am?" (Matthew 16:13ff.).

Responding to his own question, Bonhoeffer first tells us what others are saying about him. Some remark on his calm, his cheerfulness, his confidence—remarkable, they think, in the light of his actual circumstances. Look! He steps from his prison cell as though he were a country squire! Others tell of his outstanding kindness and thoughtfulness to people, including the prison guards, with whom he speaks in a friendly and free way "as though it were [his] to command." Some also note the patience and equability with which the young prisoner faces the "misfortune" that has come upon him. This proud upper-class intellectual (at Union Seminary in the early '30s some thought him insufferable, haughty!), this scholar and professor already famous though not yet forty: how astonishing it is, they say, that he can endure this humiliation with such dignity?

But then the poet reveals the darkness and the terror that reside in his own soul. Much as he would like to, he cannot trust the fine reports of others. They may attribute to him wonderfully noble virtues, but within himself he knows the spiritual warfare, the duplicity, and the anguish that prey upon him. In reality, he is "weary and empty at praying, at thinking, at making." He feels that he has been beaten already—like a defeated army "fleeing in disorder."

Who really, then, is he? The brave believer others say that he is, or the "woe-begone weakling" he so often feels himself to be?

In the end, Bonhoeffer confesses, he can only leave the assessment of his life to his Creator: "Whoever I am, <u>Thou</u> knowest, O God, I am thine."[12]

---

12. The quotations are from the original translation of Bonhoeffer's German by J. B. Leishmen, and are found in many places, including the first translation of *The Cost of Discipleship* to appear in the English-speaking world, which was published by the S.C.M. Press of London in 1948; pp. 15–16.

As I consider the words that Bob Miller wrote about himself during his final hours (his obituary), I often find myself thinking of Bonhoeffer's moving poem:

> Miller, *The Rev. Robert Whiteley*
>
> —*in his 84th year. He was active with the Untied Church of Canada, the Student Christian Movement, the S.C.M. Book room, the Bob Miller Book Room. He is survived by the four families of his brother Douglas. He has been supported by many of the choicest friends and his companion of 50 years Paul Warner.*

It may be conjecture, it may be projection, it may be exaggeration or simply making more of the recorded data than it can bear, but what I hear in that simple, frustratingly factual, self-composed obituary seems to me *Bob's* way of saying, in another, hidden manner, precisely the sort of thing that Dietrich Bonhoeffer concludes in this poem about the identity and meaning of his own life. There was no need, really, for Robert Whiteley Miller to name himself "The Rev." or to allude to his ordination in a church that he rarely attended any more; there was even less need for him to remind the world of his work with the SCM, which ended so painfully. At very least, the obituary makes it plain for all to see that this many-sided and multitalented man, with his knowledge of contemporary literature and art, his rapt involvement with the art and culture of the orient, and the various involvements and rich relationships of his past and present still considered himself a Christian minister. "*Whoever I am, Thou knowest, O God, I am thine!*"

And that is how I, too, am content to remember him. I think I shall not meet his like again. May his beloved, "Kierkegaardian" spirit rest in the great and peace-filled silence that "passeth understanding."

Acknowledgments

SEVERAL PERSONS HELPED AND encouraged me in the preparation of this work. I am particularly grateful to Mary McInroy, a second cousin of Bob Miller, for providing me not only with some of the letters that she received from Bob over the years, but also with memories of his parents and of their happy family occasions. Paul Warner, Bob's faithful friend for half a century, was very generous in sharing with me insights and information that only he could have known. From my very good friend, the late Margaret (Meg) Young, who was one of Bob Miller's oldest acquaintances, I learned many useful bits of information about Bob's student and seminary days just prior to my meeting with both of them in 1948. Meg died in April 2010, at age eighty-nine, while this book was being written. I am also very grateful to Richard Allen, a dedicated SC-Mer who met Bob shortly after his return to Canada in 1951. The first draft of Dick's important book *The Social Passion* was written at Howland House. I am indebted as well to Evelyn Reid, whose late husband, Douglas, graduated from Emmanuel College when Bob did, and who had been close to Bob Miller ever since; to the late John Coleman, who with his late wife, Marie-Jeanne de Haller Coleman, was a long-time friend and supporter of Bob Miller; and to William Fennell, emeritus professor of Christian theology at Emmanuel, who remembers Bob as "the quiet Kiekegaardian." Professor Fennell died while this manuscript was being written.

Margaret Prang, Canadian historian, whose books Bob admired and who represents the very best of the Canadian SCM, was particularly helpful and encouraging. I appreciated as well the support of Sheila McDonough of Concordia University, who was for a time one of Bob's co-workers at the SCM Book Room, as was her late brother, Bart. I am grateful to Ms. Karen Wishart, librarian of Emmanuel College, for technical data about Bob's years in that institution; and to my McGill colleague, Gerbern Oegema, for translating the article on Ellen Flesseman-van Leer. As always I am indebted to Rhoda Palfrey Hall, my wife, who worked with Bob on the national staff of the SCM from 1954 to 1957, and who read this account many times in its various drafts, made suggestions and corrections, and, as always, provided the stimulation that its author still needs despite his long experience of writing things.